California Lawmaker (2021 Edition)
The Men and Women of the California State Legislature

BY

Alexander C. Vassar

Edited by Jane Vassar

Foreword by Assemblyman Mike Gatto (Ret.)

For Sammy and Bobby

The future is still yours.

Table of Contents

Foreword
Assemblyman Mike Gatto (Ret.)

During my second term in the Legislature, I presided over Assembly sessions as Assistant Speaker Pro Tempore. As such, I had the opportunity to soak in the knowledge and wisdom of E. Dotson Wilson, the long-serving (and truly iconic) Chief Clerk of the Assembly. During one such study session, he made one of several points that has stuck with me ever since.

"You know," he said, "despite being a state since 1850 – despite term limits – despite California's huge population – less than 4,000 people have had the honor of serving in the California Legislature." He elaborated, "There have been about 3,000 Assemblymembers, and the total of State Senators still numbers in the hundreds."

Now I must confess that I didn't believe him at the time. There was simply no way that in a state as big as California, with so much turnover in the last couple generations, there had been such a small number of lawmakers. However, he was correct.

I tell this story to make two points. First, to serve in the California Legislature is indeed a select honor. Perhaps if more people treated it as such, both outside the Legislature and inside, our state would be better off.

And to honor something, you need institutional knowledge – the kind that is conveyed in a book like this. Second, there is just one person in the world who knows as much about the Legislature as Dotson Wilson. That is Alex Vassar, the author of this book. Indeed, where else could one go to verify the statistics Dotson cited? And with Dotson now retired, much of the heavy mantle of California history rests on Mr. Vassar's shoulders.

Why study the California Legislature? To many readers, the answers are obvious. First, California is a big state, and what happens here matters. Indeed, as I saw so many times during my legislative tenure, "As California

1

goes, so goes the nation." But even putting aside legislative trends, California's lawmakers have always been a microcosm for the evolution of the United States. During the early days of statehood, it was common to see lawmakers born in Germany or Ireland. Recently, we have had lawmakers born in Guatemala and the Philippines. To study the past is to know the future. To study the California Legislature is to understand the rich complexity of one of the world's most fascinating societies.

I hope you enjoy this book as much as I did.

May the institutional knowledge it transmits make California a better place.

Assemblyman Mike Gatto (Ret.)
43rd District
June 2010 – December 2016

Why Study the Legislature?

"Laws hammered out on an anvil of honest differences of opinion are bound to be more equitable than those dictated by tyrannical authority, and those of us who have had the privilege of forging some of the laws under which we live have gained more than we realize from the experience."
- *Former Assemblyman Sam Yorty[1]*

California's Legislature and the people who have served in it have an amazingly rich history. Some have held positions of national importance like Secretary of Defense Caspar Weinberger or U.S. Supreme Court Justices Joseph McKenna and Stephen J. Field (all of whom served in the Assembly).

Not all these stories end well: California legislators have also been fatally wounded in a bar brawl[2] or died in a drunken canoeing accident[3]. Assemblyman Frank M. Pixley, "posed as a California Senator so he could ride side by side with General Ulysses S. Grant at the Battle of Cold Harbor" in 1864[4].

California is a land of diverse climates and people, and draws inhabitants from all over the world. The story of the legislature is a microcosm of these fascinating people and will fascinate you if you let it.

---

[1] Sam Yorty. Letter to Nelson S. Dilworth. Undated. From the Dilworth Collection.
[2] After killing Assemblyman Charles Piercy in a duel, Assembly Speaker pro Tem Daniel Showalter fled the state. Years later, Showalter moved to Mexico, where he died in 1866 of lockjaw resulting from a fight at a bar he owned in Mazatlan. Source: "DEATH OF COL. SHOWALTER" Mariposa Free Press, 10 March 1866. 1. California Digital Newspaper Collection. Web. Accessed 12 December 2016.
[3] George N. McConaha drowned in a canoe accident off Vashon Island. The book History of the State of Washington by Edmond Stephen Meany (Macmillan Company; 1909) notes that McConaha had been drinking prior to his canoe trip, and that his canoe "overturned in a storm..."
[4] "Attorney General Frank M. Pixley." California Department of Justice, 2017, caag.state.ca.us/ag/history/8pixley.htm.

The second floor Rotunda of the nearly empty California State Capitol in May.
Photo courtesy Sarah Couch.

Annus Horribilis

"It has been a very painful and difficult year. We have endured something unparalleled in our history and we did it exceptionally well."
- Assembly Speaker Anthony Rendon[5]

In Latin, the term annus horribilis means "horrible year." For the California state legislature, the year 2020 was that in generous portions.

Last Night of Session 2019

The last week of session is usually a tense evening as bills are exchanged between the two houses and compromises are worked out to gain last-minute passage, leading up to a flurry of activity on the final night that frequently leaks into the early hours of the following morning.

The final week of the 2019 session was particularly tense, with large crowds gathering to oppose legislation requiring the Department of Public Health to annually review immunization reports from schools and institutions to identify physicians and surgeons who submitted five or more medical exemption forms each year. The bill, authored by Senator and pediatrician Richard Pan, was the latest in a series that Pan had authored to ensure that students in public schools had been vaccinated against common illnesses.

After a series of contentious committee hearings, the bill was presented to Governor Newsom, who signed it on September 9th. In the days that followed, increasing numbers of protesters occupied the hallways of the building, promising to stay until the law was repealed.

At 5:14 PM on the final night of session in 2019, as the Senate was working through the final rush of bills, a visitor sitting in the gallery of the Senate chambers yelled "That's for the dead babies!" and threw a

---

[5] Tweet by Hannah Wiley of the Sacramento Bee (@hannahcwiley) 9/1/2020
https://twitter.com/hannahcwiley/status/1300707626599067649

container filled with blood down onto the Senate Floor, where it splashed onto Senators Galgiani, Glazer, Hurtado, Mitchell, Rubio, and Skinner.

The Senate promptly adjourned for three and a half hours, before reconvening in a fourth-floor committee room (because the Senate Floor had been declared a crime scene and closed for investigation by the California Highway Patrol). At the time, many longtime staff agreed that 2019 was the craziest end of session they'd ever seen.

The Coronavirus Closure

Although I didn't know it at the time, March 12th would be my last visit to the building in 2020. Walking through the halls, I noticed a slight tension, with people moving more quickly through the hallways than usual. I also noticed that, in addition to the "This office does not accept gifts" signs, there were a large number of doors with "No offense but we don't shake hands" advisories posted.

A day later, on the afternoon of March 13th, California State Parks announced that it would be "temporarily suspending all guided tours at the California State Capitol Museum." Almost immediately, the Joint Rules Committee emailed legislative staff that "the Capitol Building will be closed this weekend, except for staff presenting badges. If you plan to come into the Capitol Building on Saturday and/or Sunday, please have your ID badge."

After an uneasy weekend, the dam broke on Monday, March 16th. That morning, seven counties in the San Francisco Bay Area declared public health emergencies requiring seven million Californians to remain at home except for medical appointments or food runs to restaurants and grocery stores.

That afternoon, the Senators quickly approved Senate Resolution 86, creating a new rule for that house which permits Senators to attend committee hearings and floor sessions remotely by telephone, teleconference, or other electronic means.

The first floor hallway of the California State Capitol on May 4, 2020.
Photo by Brian Ebbert

It's hard to overstate how significant a departure this was from the customs of the usually traditional State Senate. Previously the Senate Rules required that votes of lawmakers would not be counted if they were not standing on the red carpet of the senate floor itself. One incident from the prior decade had seen the presiding officer refuse to count a vote which Senator Jeff Denham had called out from the Gallery.

The night ended with both houses passing Assembly Concurrent Resolution 189, which sent both houses of the legislature into a recess for nearly a month.

The following day, March 17th, the Joint Rules Committee issued a statement to legislative staff saying that "the State Capitol Building and the [Legislative Office Building] are closed to the public, effective March

Footprints identify where visitors to the Capitol should stand to maintain social distance during summer 2020.

18, 2020, until further notice. If you have essential government business to conduct, you will need your Legislative ID badge to access the building."

On April 3rd, it was announced that Senate President pro Tem Atkins and Assembly Speaker Rendon were postponing the legislature's return to Sacramento until May 4th. Looking back on the history of the California legislature, I had to go back nearly 160 years to find another long-term closure of the Capitol.

The Flood of 1862

In January 1862, following a series of major rain storms which left Sacramento flooded under several feet of water, the legislature temporarily adjourned to permit the relocation of Capitol to San Francisco for the duration of that session. Several members of the legislature were quarantined with symptoms during the global influenza pandemic in 1919. The legislature briefly discussed adjourning but elected to continue meeting while providing for daily disinfectant of the state capitol building.

More recently, in January 2001 the State Capital was struck by a semi-truck, starting a raging fire directly beneath the Senate Chambers and causing $12 million in damage. Even with the smell of smoke still in the halls, the State Senate didn't miss a beat and held a floor session less than 10 hours later, meeting instead on the Assembly Floor.

On the evening of March 19th, Governor Newsom issued executive order N-33-20 to enforce the order by the California State Public Health Officer requiring all Californians to stay home with limited exceptions. The order went into effect on the same day and would remain in place until further notice.

On July 2nd, the legislature adjourned for a Summer Recess and on the following Monday the State Capitol was closed for a cleaning of Assembly offices and common spaces. When the legislature resumed on July 27th, each Senator was limited to one staffer in the office.

The August Lightning Siege

At the same time that Senate pro Tem Atkins was working hard to keep the Senate on track for the impending end of session, the next natural disaster was building 1,000 miles to the south.

On August 16th, a small tropical depression grew just strong enough to become a tropical storm for about twelve hours before losing strength and becoming a tropical depression again. The atmospheric pressures created by this storm interacted with the weather over California, creating a massive lightning storm that covered much of the state.

As the storm moved up the state, scientists recorded over 12,000 lightning strikes throughout Northern California, sparking nearly 600 wildfires including what would become three of the four largest fires in modern state history. For more than a month after the storm, much of the state was caught in thick smoke as fires burned through more than two and a half million acres.

End of Session 2020

On Wednesday, August 26th, it was announced that Senator Brian Jones, who had attended the floor session on Monday, had tested positive for SARS-CoV-2. Because Senator Jones had attended a lunch with nearly all members of the Senate Republican Caucus the day before, all Republican Senators except Jim Nielsen were required to be tested before being permitted to return for another floor session. Instead, they were to be connected to the session via internet connection for their Sacramento apartments or homes in their districts.

Unfortunately, as happened so often in the lives of Californians in 2020, technical difficulties (preventing the connecting of the laptops) weren't able to be resolved for a full day. This meant that ten Republican Senators, representing a quarter of the state's population, were unable to join the session because they couldn't physically attend (because of their quarantine) while the technical issues prevented their remote attendance.

Assemblyman Santiago, chair of the Assembly Committee on Communications and Conveyance, listens as Consumer Reports CA lobbyist Maureen Mahoney testifies remotely from a nearby Witness Videoconference Room during the May 5th hearing in the Assembly Chambers.   *Photo by Brian Ebbert*

Clearly frustrated, Senator Chang said "Today, despite my cautious actions, my fellow caucus members and I were denied the right to vote on over 30 bills and appointments... Californians deserve representation in the Senate regardless of party affiliation. To forbid an entire caucus from voting when all members were exposed defies logic and robs my constituents of their voice."

On Friday, August 28th, history was made again when the State Senate permitted remote voting during a floor session for the first time. With two Senators participating remotely from home in their districts, the

Senate session on August 28, 2020 was the first time California legislators cast floor votes from outside Sacramento since 1862[6].

Three days later, with the most turbulent session in generations behind them, the legislature had managed to pass more than four hundred bills, of which 372 were signed into law by Governor Newsom. This was the fewest new laws to come out of a regular session year since 1901[7].

---

[6] With the exception of two ceremonial one-day sessions in 1950 and 2000 when the legislature returned to the former state capitol at Benicia.

[7] This does not include the meetings of the legislature in the even-year "budget sessions" between 1948 and 1966 when the legislature met only to approve the state budget and budget-related bills (rather than approving general legislation).

The New Session

> "I suppose swearing-in ceremonies are simple rituals and nothing more. The justification for them is not just the literal promise that you make --it's to impress you with the formality of the occasion and your responsibility."
> - State Senator John F. Dunlap[8]

The 2020 election was long and challenging, with legislators being forced to find new ways to campaign in an environment where large public events were prohibited and voters weren't interested in coming face-to-face with campaign workers.

With the loss of two seats in the Senate, the Republican membership in the legislature now have a combined 28 members, just under a quarter of the legislature.

State Senate	State Assembly
30 Democrats	60 Democrats
9 Republicans	19 Republicans
1 Vacancy	1 No Party Preference

The thirty Democrats in the Senate[9] are just below their all-time high of 32 in the 1883 Regular Session and are the largest majority caucus since the Republicans held 35 Senate seats in 1933.

Last session, the eleven Senate Republicans had the smallest caucus since 1961. This year, at nine members, the caucus is the smallest it has been since 1861, when only six Republicans served in the upper house[10]. The only exception has been the sessions of 1863-1868, when the

---

[8] Senator from Napa by John F. Dunlap (senatorfromnapa.com/). Chapter 1.

[9] The session started with thirty Democrats, nine Republicans, and one vacancy resulting from the resignation of Senator Holly Mitchell.

[10] California's Legislature (California State Printer; 2016) by E. Dotson Wilson, Brian S. Ebbert. Appendix O, page 335.

Republicans (including Abraham Lincoln seeking reelection as President) ran under the "Union" party label.

Former Republican Chad Mayes' victory in 2020 made him the first person elected to the State Assembly without a party affiliation since the 1940s[11]. It hadn't been nearly as long in the Senate, where several Senators in the 1980s had been elected to terms as independents. The most recent was Senator Quentin L. Kopp of San Francisco in 1994.

Freshman Assemblyman Alex T. Lee, sworn into office at age 25, is the youngest legislator since Maurice E. Atkinson served a single Assembly term in 1939. Atkinson declined a second term in 1940 to run for Congress. At the other end of the spectrum is Senator Bob Archuleta, first elected to the Senate in 2018 at age 73, who was the oldest freshman since Assemblyman Albert I. Stewart (age 74) was inaugurated in January 1945.

Speakers in the Senate

Two former Assembly Speakers (Toni Atkins and Robert Hertzberg) are now serving in the Senate. Before Hertzberg, the last former Speaker to serve in the State Senate was Frank F. Merriam in 1929-1931. The last time that multiple former Speakers served in the Senate together was 1876-1877, when Speakers James Farley and George H. Rogers served together. Also in the Senate with Farley and Rogers was Robert Howe, who would become Assembly Speaker more than a decade later[12].

Longest serving

The longest serving current legislator is Senator Jim Nielsen, who was first elected to the Legislature in 1978[13]. To provide some perspective on how long ago that was, consider this; 14 current Assemblymembers and 5

---

[11] Ralph A. Beal was elected to his only Assembly term in 1944 as an Independent. Beal, a great-great-grandnephew of Benjamin Franklin, ran for a second term in 1946 as a Democrat and lost.

[12] Speakership dates from California's Legislature (California State Printer; 2006) by Wilson and Ebbert.

[13] Nielsen's service has not been continuous. He was out of office from 1990 to 2006.

Senators were born after Nielsen's first election to the Senate. That's not the record though. In 1998, when Ralph Dills finished his final term in the Senate, 87 of his fellow legislators had been born after he first assumed office.

Birthplace

At the start of the current session, 75 California-born legislators are joined by 31 members from other states, and 13 from foreign countries[14]. Of the other states, Ohio and Pennsylvania lead the list with four members each followed by New York and Texas with three. The rise of Pennsylvania has been an anomaly, with New Yorkers usually being the largest group of non-Californians. A decade ago New York led with seven members and there were only two Pennsylvanians in the two houses.

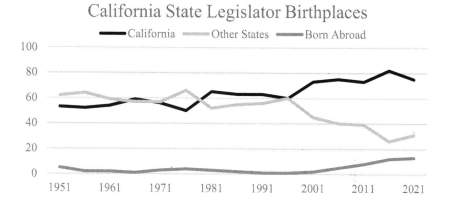

California State Legislator Birthplaces

Former Members

As of early 2021, there are approximately 440 living former legislators. The oldest is former Senator John F. Dunlap, who turned 98 in late 2020 and the youngest is former Assemblyman Sebastian Ridley-Thomas (33 years old) who served from 2013 to 2018.

---

[14] The eleven countries are Canada, China, El Salvador, France, Germany, Iran, Mexico, Philippines, South Korea, and Vietnam. There's another who was born on a U.S. base in Japan,

Legislator Statistics by Decade of First Service

Decade	[New Legislators] Men	Women	Average Age	Avg Service	Currently In Office
1850s	721	-	34.3[15]	1.7 years	-
1860s	599	-	37.7[16]	2.4 years	-
1870s	296	-	44.1[17]	2.9 years	-
1880s	476	-	42.0[18]	3.0 years	-
1890s	379	-	41.2[19]	3.1 years	-
1900s	327	-	39.1[20]	3.9 years	-
1910s	282	4	42.4[21]	4.9 years	-
1920s	177	2	42.1	7.0 years	-
1930s	189	2	43.1	7.5 years	-
1940s	123	1	43.6	9.5 years	-
1950s	109	3	43.9	9.9 years	-
1960s	117	2	41.5	11.1 years	-
1970s	103	11	40.8	11.4 years	1
1980s	64	13	42.3	10.2 years	-
1990s	105	42	46.5	7.5 years	3
2000s	103	42	48.1	7.2 years	5
2010s	107	45	46.4	5.4 years	97
2020s	9	4	54.6	-	13

New Legislators: The number of legislators serving first terms in each decade.
Average Age: The age of the decade's new legislators when assuming office.
Currently in Office: Calculated as of the first day of the 2021-22 regular session.

---

[15] Research has identified birthyears for 51% of new 1850s members.
[16] Research has identified birthyears for 70% of new 1860s members.
[17] Research has identified birthyears for 99% of new 1870s members.
[18] Research has identified birthyears for 93% of new 1880s members.
[19] Research has identified birthyears for 89% of new 1890s members.
[20] Research has identified birthyears for 91% of new 1900s members.
[21] Research has identified birthyears for 95% of new 1910s members.

Legislators by Decade

"I wish that your constituents, all of them, could look at you through the critical eyes of this old "pro" and say, 'You have proven worthy, and our State is better off because of the sacrifices that you have made for it.'"
- Assemblyman Don A. Allen[22]

The first decade of California statehood was a wild one. It was the decade with the youngest legislators who served for the shortest periods. The gold fields and enterprise called and it was hard for the legislature to recruit and retain experienced members. Assembly terms were originally just one year (Senators were elected to two year terms) and few returned for additional terms.

It was over half a century before most state legislators started serving more than four years. As the decades passed, California voters gradually began electing older legislators who stayed longer. Between the 1850s and the arrival of term limits in 1990, the average length of time served by legislators grew every decade.

While term limits didn't increase the number of new legislators arriving in the legislature[23], it did ensure more consistent turnover of seats, dramatically decreasing the institutional knowledge by removing senior lawmakers.

Two of the most significant changes that term limits brought were the election of more female lawmakers and an increase in the average age of new members.

---

[22] Don A. Allen, Sr. Letter to Nelson S. Dilworth. 18 June 1959. From the Dilworth Collection.

[23] In its first three decades, term limits resulted in an average of two fewer new legislators per decade compared to the years between the start of the Progressive Era (in 1911) and the start of term limits (in 1990).

The California State Capitol following
an unusual hail storm in February 2018.

The Capitol

> **"There is no danger of Sacramento washing away.**
> **This building never will be washed away."**
> *– Constitutional Convention Delegate John T. Wickes*[24]

The California State Capitol is a fascinating place filled with contrasts. In the 1950s-era Annex, young staffers sip coffee while tweeting or browsing news online. On the other side of the building, where construction began while Lincoln was President, you can walk through rooms appearing exactly as they did a century ago. Similarly, although the building appears imposing and unchanging on the outside, plans are underway to dramatically change the way in which the legislators and public use the building.

In the early years it wasn't always clear that Sacramento would be the state capital. After first meeting in San Jose, four other cities had their turn before Sacramento became the permanent choice. Even as late as the 1879 constitutional convention, delegates expressed concern about the city washing away in a flood or being unhealthy due to the surrounding swamps. Constitutional Convention Delegate Dennis W. Harrington noted "It is well known and it cannot be

---

[24] Debates and Proceedings of the Constitutional Convention of the State of California, Convened at the City of Sacramento, Saturday, September 29, 1878, Volume 3 (J. D. Young; 1881), page 1388.

denied, that this is not a healthy location. It is a boneyard for many of the best representatives that the people ever sent to this place."[25]

After extensive deliberations, a majority of the delegates voted to keep the Capitol in the building which convention delegate Marion Biggs described as "a credit to the State, and one that every citizen of the State should be proud of."

The Capitol was here to stay.

The Historic Capitol

First Floor

The first floor of the Historic Capitol building is a museum that includes restored offices decorated to illustrate a particular era of California history. In the Rotunda, State Parks guides and volunteers sit at a table prepared to answer your questions about the height of the dome[26] or add you to a tour group.

Exhibit rooms showcase items from the State Parks collection that explain a particular chapter from California's history. Recent exhibit themes have included the state's role in World War II and how automobiles changed the state.

Basement

One floor down from the Rotunda stands a massive bronze statue of former Governor (and President) Ronald Reagan[27]. Other spots in the basement that are open to the public include the Bill Room (where staff

---

[25] Debates and Proceedings of the Constitutional Convention of the State of California, Convened at the City of Sacramento, Saturday, September 29, 1878, Volume 3 (J. D. Young; 1881), page 1388.

[26] The ball at the very top of the Cupola is just short of 220 feet above street level.

[27] Although it had been referred to as the Capitol basement for years, reporters covering the Reagan statue dedication apparently felt that name was insufficient, and the location was referred to as the "Lower Rotunda."

and the public can request copies of legislation or related publications), a gift shop (which is one of the few places you can legally purchase copies of the state seal[28]), and a cafeteria.

Second Floor

A large part of this floor is occupied by the Senate and Assembly chambers. When visiting the Senate chambers, be sure to check out the bust of Senator David Broderick over by the outside windows[29]. In the front right corner of the Assembly Chambers, you'll be able to see two desks permanently reserved for former Speakers Jesse Unruh and Willie Brown.

One of the coolest parts of the second floor is a difficult to reach room called "The Void," which is the empty space that was left when the Annex was added onto what had been the outside of the Senate Chambers in the early 1950s. If you manage to get the door unlocked, you will see the weathered former exterior of the building which last saw the sun during the Eisenhower Administration. Other points of interest on this floor are the offices of the Assembly Speaker and Senate President pro Tem.

David Bowman of the Chief Clerk's Office speaks about the history of the legislature in the Assembly Chambers.

A little known fact is that Hanns Scharff, the mosaic artist who restored the tiles that cover most of the Second Floor during the 1980s, was a

---

[28] Government Code, Section 402(b)

[29] Broderick, by then a U.S. Senator, was killed in a duel with the Chief Justice of the California Supreme Court.

German interrogator of allied flight crews during World War II[30]. His interrogation work was studied by the U.S. government's High-Value Interrogation Group after the 9/11 attacks and his tile-work is admired daily by visitors to Capitol.

Third Floor

The smallest floor, in terms of space accessible to the public, is the third floor. Here you can find the Assembly and Senate galleries, which are almost always open to the public whenever the legislature is meeting[31]. There are also portraits of the five most recent Governors and the offices of the Senate Majority Leader, Senate Minority Leader, and Assembly Majority Leader.

Fourth Floor

The fourth floor of the historic side of the Capitol is a great place to get lost. This space, which started as an empty attic, became a storage area and was finally converted into a series of committee rooms, support offices, and long dimly-lit hallways that seem to go nowhere.

It was in these poorly lit spaces that Senate staffer Marybelle Wallace was killed on April 14, 1927[32]. Initially friendly to lobbyist Reginald "Harry" Hill, the relationship soured when Hill began to pursue Wallace romantically and asked her to marry him. Wallace declined the offer and managed to avoid him for a while, but Hill eventually found her. After Wallace again refused to marry him, Hill killed her and then shot himself.

---

[30] "FBI gets an unexpected lesson from a former interrogator for the Nazis" by Del Quentin Wilber, Los Angeles Times; 10 June 2016.

[31] For more information, see California Constitution, Article IV, Section 7 (c)

[32] "State Capitol can give you the creeps" by Greg Lucas, San Francisco Chronicle; 27 October 2002.

The Capitol Annex

Basement – An Underground Parking Lot

The basement is where the vehicles for legislators and a select senior staff are parked. It's worth mentioning that they don't actually get to park their cars themselves – the basement accommodates far more vehicles than it was originally intended to and, as a consequence, the vehicles have to be crammed into every imaginable corner. Occasionally Capitol visitors will push the wrong button on the elevator and emerge with more than a little confusion. Then a nearby Highway Patrol officer will start walking in their direction and they'll hurriedly jump back inside.

First Floor – Speed Dating for Counties

Easily the busiest floor in the Capitol, the most visible feature of the first floor annex is the county displays that line the hallways. Much like a local government speed-dating session, each of California's 58 counties is given fifteen square feet of wall space to explain who they are and why you should love them... with mixed results. Also on the First Floor are the offices for the Governor, Lieutenant Governor, and Department of Finance.

Second Floor – The Short End of the Stick

In all honesty, the second floor was probably never going to win any beauty contests. The ceilings seem lower, the hallways seem darker and, compared with the first and third floors... it's a ghost town. The one redeeming quality of the interior Assembly offices on this floor is access to a patio with picnic tables that gets direct sunlight for about an hour a day.

Third Floor – Where Business Is Done

Built at the same level as the second floor of the Historic Capitol, the third floor of the Annex is clearly where things happen. This floor is home to a number of offices that staff must visit on a regular basis (Assembly Rules Committee, Legislative Counsel, and several committee rooms) as well as several that they should visit more than they do (Assembly Chief Clerk, Secretary of the Senate, and the Sergeant-at-Arms of the two houses).

This is the floor where lobbyists congregate just off the Floor when the legislature is meeting. During the end-of-session rush, the hallways become so packed that all conversations must be yelled and the air becomes heavy and humid. If you time it right, it's worth experiencing at least once.

Fourth Floor – Offices and Committee Rooms

Aside from the legislator offices that occupy most of the floor, the defining feature of the fourth floor is the two large committee rooms that are adjacent to the Historic Capitol. In Room 4202, a larger-than-life portrait of larger-than-life former Speaker Jesse Unruh hangs behind the dais. It's easily the focal point in the room and people attending hearings often spend their time studying the picture because it is far easier to see than the actual legislators. Across the hall in Room 4203, the wall is similarly dominated by a huge Works Progress Administration (WPA) mural by Lucile Lloyd. The mural, which depicts the origins of a name "California," has looked down on more contentious bill hearings than any other piece of artwork in the state.

Fifth Floor – Offices

Two notable features stand out in my mind when thinking about the 5th floor. The first is the long sloping ramp that almost every Capitol staffer has thought about riding down on an office chair. Almost all of them rethink it when they see the security camera pointed at the bottom of the ramp; there's no way that you're not going to end up paying for this ride. Had this author ever tried it, it's likely that he would have injured a leg when he crashed into a recycling bin outside of the Senate Budget Committee office. But he certainly didn't, so I guess we'll never know.

At the top of that ramp is one of the hidden jewels of the State Capitol; the branch office of the State Library's California Research Bureau (CRB). Inside this small office, you will find friendly staff that can answer questions, help conduct research, and can offer some fantastic book recommendations[33].

---

[33] Maybe they'll recommend this exact book (if they think you're cool enough).

Sixth Floor – Wait, There's A Sixth Floor?

Yes, there is a sixth floor. About half the floor is member offices, with the remainder being bathrooms, a cafeteria, and a hallway to the 4th Floor of the Historic Capitol.

Columbus and Isabella Have Left the Building

On July 7, 2020, a statuary group titled "Columbus' Last Appeal to Queen Isabella" was removed from the center of the Capitol Rotunda, which it had occupied for decades. The statue depicts Queen Isabella I of Castile approving the funding for Christopher Columbus first voyage. On the base of the statue was the inscription;

> "I will assume the undertaking," she said, "for my own crown of Castille, and am ready to pawn my jewels to defray the expenses of it, if the funds in the treasury shall be found inadequate."

Presented to the State of California by Darius Ogden Mills in 1883, the statue had occupied the center of the Rotunda for generations.

For years, the statue had played a central role in the trips to the Capitol by schoolkids and tourists. It was in the center of an easily identifiable part of the Capitol just feet from the tables where visitors can sign up for tours from State Parks guides. To the legislative staff and lobbyists who were in the building on a more regular basis, the statue was just a part of the background, with the exception of the longstanding traditional tossing of pennies on the last night of session.

Legislative staffers would toss pennies from the second floor of the rotunda, trying to land the coin in Isabella's crown without it bouncing out. According to the tradition, a staffer who accomplished the rare feat was guaranteed to have their most important bills pass.

The tradition, rarely discussed with outsiders because we all understood how silly it was, existed for years before it was thrust into the spotlight. On one morning in 2014, after a late night session, it was discovered that

(Above) Queen Isabella with a penny visible in her crown. (Below) The page's hand with broken finger visible. *Photos courtesy Tyson Dekker.*

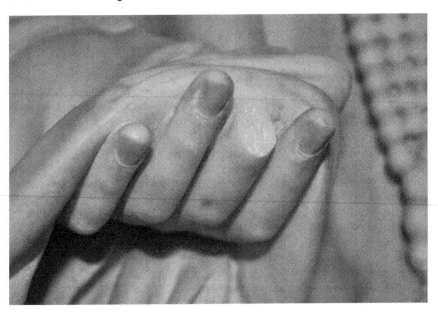

one of the fingers on Queen Isabella's pageboy had broken off. The discovery ignited a massive controversy, with most suspicion being placed on a falling penny pitched by a legislative staffer. Many legislative staff privately shared theories that the blame more likely belonged to an accidental bump from a tourist getting too close to the statue in order to get a great picture of the rotunda ceiling above.

As it turned out, the Page's finger had broken off a number of times, apparently the first time coming less than fifteen years after the statue was installed at the Capitol.

> *"It was thought at first that the loss of the page's fingers might have been accidental, but the State Janitor said this afternoon that if this were the case the pieces should have been found in the railed inclosure which the group occupies. No such pieces have been found..."*[34]

The finger was apparently found, because again went missing in 1937...

> *"Captain Joe Beard of the state capitol police intends to "put the finger" on a page boy—if and when he finds it. The finger involved is from the group of statuary in the capitol rotunda depicting Columbus appearing before the court of Queen Isabella of Spain."*[35]

The statue was removed from the Rotunda in July 1976 and relocated to the nearby State Treasurer's building as part of the preparations for the large-scale restoration of the Capitol that lasted until 1981. During the relocation of the statue, the inevitable happened...

> *"The pro-statue people finally won, and Chris and Izzy were moved back from the lobby of a state building across the street*

---

[34] "Columbus' Last Appeal Defaced: Statuary Group at the Capitol Injured," San Francisco Call; 21 January 1899, page 5.

[35] "Statue's Missing Finger Is Sought," Calexico Chronicle; 10 September 1937, page 4.

at a cost of $37,000. The only casualty was the page, who had the index finger on his right hand broken off."[36]

They say history repeats itself, and it appears the finger was again found, because it fell off again in 2014[37].

"This much is not in doubt: Sometime Friday or Saturday, part of a finger from the marble statue depicting Queen Isabella and Christopher Columbus in the Capitol rotunda broke off. A tourist discovered the detached digit Saturday afternoon…"

This time, the blame was placed on a long-standing tradition of casting pennies into Isabella's crown on the last night of session.

The History of the Coin-Toss

Although the practice of tossing pennies into the Isabella's crown apparently predated the 1976 move to the Treasurer's Building, the end of session coin-toss, described in an essay by long-time Capitol staffer Peter Detwiler as "pitching pennies into Queen Izzy's hat" began again in the mid-1980s when Fred Silva (Chief Fiscal Advisor to Senator David Roberti), Jesse Huff (Director of Finance), and Dave Doerr (Chief Consultant to the Assembly Ways and Means Committee) were standing "at the railing talking about some budget deal and one of us starting tossing pennies into Izzy's crown."

Over time, Capitol staff who had a few years' experience figured out that the pennies most likely to stay put in the crown were those made before 1982[38].

---

[36] "Chris and Izzy Return to the Rotunda" by Steve Wiegand, San Francisco Chronicle; 13 October 1982, page 34

[37] "Broken finger on statue in California Capitol rotunda follows late-night coin toss," by Jim Miller and Claudia Buck, Sacramento Bee; 2 September 2014.

[38] Until 1982, pennies were made almost entirely of copper and weighed 3.11 grams. Pennies made since 1983 are made almost entirely of zinc and therefore weigh less (they weigh 2.5 grams) and are far more likely to bounce off the

After the broken finger of 2014, signs were posted announcing that the Highway Patrol would be keeping an eye on the statue during late night sessions and anyone caught throwing pennies would face serious consequences. Allegedly, the few staffers who continued to pitch pennies late into the evening on the last night of session were always prepared to run (at a moment's notice) to the Senate Floor if "the Law" suddenly appeared.

The Curtain Falls on Chris and Izzy

On June 16, 2020, Senate President pro Tempore Toni G. Atkins, Assembly Speaker Anthony Rendon (D-Lakewood), and Assembly Rules Committee Chair Ken Cooley issued a statement announcing the removal of the statue from the Rotunda:

> *"Christopher Columbus is a deeply polarizing historical figure given the deadly impact his arrival in this hemisphere had on indigenous populations. The continued presence of this statue in California's Capitol, where it has been since 1883, is completely out of place today. It will be removed."*

The removal of the statue was completed on the morning of July 7th and the newly empty Capitol Rotunda means that there are some new options for the use of the space. Notable Californians have lain in state in the current Capitol fewer than ten times, beginning with former State Senator James W. Coffroth in 1872. In modern times, the most recent legislators to lie in state in the Rotunda were Assemblyman B. T. Collins (1993) and Congressman Robert Matsui (2005). Will the practice of prominent Californians lying in state make a comeback? Only the future can tell.

---

marble and out of the crown... allegedly... clearly the author is not the type of person who would ever test such a thing.

The Swing Space

In the decades since the Capitol Annex was added onto the original Capitol in the 1950s, it has gradually become less and less functional. Originally constructed in an age when telephone booths were a necessity, it has been modernized over the years to meet new technology and security requirements with holes drilled between floors to run internet cables and the enclosed security "sunrooms" added after the 9/11 attacks.

Today, the largest modernization of State Capitol workspace since the 1950s is underway. Just south of the Capitol, on the other side of N Street behind the Legislative Office Building, construction is underway on 10-floor Capitol Annex Swing Space Building. This tower will house 1,200+ staff from the legislative and executive branches while the State Capitol's current Annex is demolished and a new one constructed over the next few years.

The work to rebuild the Capitol is being led by someone who is remarkably well prepared for the job. Although most people run for the legislature for the chance to write laws, Assemblyman Ken Cooley likely ran to spend his time in office rebuilding California's living monument to democracy and representative government.

A longtime legislative staffer who gave frequent tours of the Capitol, Cooley is leading the effort in his role as Chairman of the legislature's Joint Rules Committee. During the restoration of the historic side of the State Capitol in 1975 to 1982, Cooley (then a young staffer) helped oversee the project as Chief of Staff to Assemblyman Lou Papan, who was then the Chair of Joint Rules Committee.

Spend a few minutes talking with Cooley about the project and you will likely walk away with both a handful of material outlining the sweeping vision for the project as well as the clear impression that Cooley sees the building with almost the familiarity and affection that you'd expect for a close friend who is in the hospital with a serious, but curable, condition.

It won't be easy project to complete. It's not easy to negotiate the balance between public access to the "people's house" and the security needs of the most populous state but this project is the job Cooley has been preparing for decades to tackle.

The Capitol Annex Swing Space Building under construction in early 2020.

The author is grateful to Adela Freeman, a great-great-great-granddaughter of D. O. Mills, for sharing her family's documents relating to the history of the Columbus statue.

Senate first Senators 1961-2021 (by Session)

Senate First

One of the traits that defined the relationship between the houses for many years was the relatively small number of Senators whose legislative service had begun in the Assembly. The Senate, whose members were drawn largely from rural counties until 1966, had a majority of Senate-only membership for much of the 1940s to mid-1960s. During that time, the Senate and Assembly were roughly equal in political power, with the Senate sometimes being seen as more powerful due to its more experienced and relatively more-powerful members.

The impact of the Unruh Speakership and the 1965 redistricting redefined that relationship for the next half-century. As Assembly Speaker, Jesse Unruh consolidated the power of that house behind himself (and it has largely remained with the Speaker since). At the same time, the forced redistricting led to more urban Senate districts and forced a number of Senators from office, while their replacements moved up from the Assembly.

After the sudden drop in 1967, the number of inter-house transfers continued to grow steadily until the late 2000s when only two Senators remained (Jeff Denham and Alex Padilla) with no Assembly experience. The 2010 election brought the first increase in the number of Senate-only members in more than two decades, a trend that has continued since.

There are now 19 Senators for whom the Senate was their house of origin and the trend indicates that they could regain a majority in the next session or two.

By 1941, Eleanor Miller, the legislature's fifth woman, was both the
State Assembly's longest-serving member as well as the only woman.
Photo from "Eleanor Miller" poster by the State Senate (1942)

Women in the Legislature

*"In preparing for today, I took the time to read the remarks
of previous Speakers who outlined their hopes and dreams
for what they wanted for our great state... I realized most of
the messages are the same—packaged differently,
articulately presented, but really the same."*
- *Senate President pro Tem Toni Atkins*[39]

On the first day of the 2021-22 Regular Session, there were 38 women serving as legislators in the two houses, the highest number in California history[40]. This is a remarkable turnaround from just four years ago, which started with the fewest female members in more than twenty years.

Of all women to serve in the legislature, the longest service was that of Senator Teresa Hughes, who served over 25 years between the two houses. The shortest service by a female legislator was Senator Vanessa Delgado, who served 110 days in 2018 before her term ended.

Senator Delgado's abbreviated term in the legislature came in large part to a curiously timed special election that resulted in her winning the special election but not the concurrently-scheduled primary for the new term beginning November 30th. Delgado's Senate District 32 in 2018 was the first time in state history that three Senators have represented a single seat in one calendar year.

Tony Mendoza held the seat until his resignation in late February and Senator Delgado assumed office in early August, serving until the end of the term on November 30. Bob J. Archuleta, who won the General Election, began his service on December 3rd.

---

[39] Assembly Daily Journal, 12 May 2014, page 4887
[40] There was also a vacancy resulting from the resignation of Holly Mitchell, who was elected to the Los Angeles County Board of Supervisors in November 2020.

Although Senator Delgado was the shortest-serving State Senator in more than a century[41], she used her time effectively, serving through the busy end of session and authoring two bills, one of which was signed by Governor Brown.

She Stood Alone

Rose Ann Vuich is frequently remembered for her time as the only female Senator in 1977-1978. During that session, she famously rang a bell whenever any other Senator referred to the house using a male pronoun. In the decades before, three earlier women whose unique roles have been largely lost to history, served as the sole member of their gender in the entire legislature.

The first four women were elected to the legislature for the 1919 session, growing to five in 1923. Ten years after the election of the first women, Assemblywoman Cora Woodbridge was defeated in her bid for a fourth term, leaving Eleanor Miller as the final woman in the legislature. After two years as the only female in the legislature, she had become the longest-serving female legislator in state history, a title she held until 1973.

Assemblywoman Miller served continuously from 1923 to 1942, including as the sole woman again from 1933 to 1936. She retired at the end of the 1942 session. After her death a year later, she was remembered on the Assembly Floor with a eulogy;

> *"It is given to few Legislators to serve for two decades in the lawmaking chambers of any State. Only one woman has been so honored by her fellow citizens and it has been the great privilege of this Assembly from 1922 to 1942 to be graced by the presence of the late Honorable Eleanor Miller...*
>
> *No Member of this Assembly was more highly esteemed by its membership, no member was ever more faithful in attendance upon her duties. No matter how long the hours, no matter how*

---

[41] Of the 11 State Senators who served for a shorter term, the most recent was Orrin Z. Hubbell, a Republican who served 15 weeks in 1903 before he died.

great the strain, her gentle presence was always here and her persuasive words of wisdom kindly given for the benefit of us all...

Her eloquent voice was often raised in this chamber in behalf of her sisters, the women of California. Many just and wise statutes of this State are the work of her legislative career in behalf of the members of her sex... No longer will her persuasive words fall on our ears, but the inspiration of her memory will linger with each of us through the years to encourage us to noble kindly deeds[42].

An interesting note is that during the year between leaving the legislature and her death, Miller apparently had dreams of returning to the Capitol. Early in 1943, the Assembly Journal published a letter from Miller to Willis Sargent, on the day he took office representing the district she had previously held;

"In imagination I was with you all on yesterday throughout the proceedings. Last night I dreamed that I went back to visit. But, like Rip Van Winkle, no one knew me and I knew no one. I went to my old seat and the man sitting there said "Are you the woman who used to sit here?" When I replied "Yes," his response was "My Lord!"[43]

The 1943 session also saw the arrival of the second woman to serve alone. The ninth female to serve in the legislature did so after her husband ran first, and lost his race. Charles Niehouse ran for Assembly in 1936 and lost by a significant margin. Six years later, his wife Kathryn ran for the same seat, narrowly unseating the candidate who had defeated her husband. After two years in office, Niehouse easily won reelection with nearly 90% of the vote.

Her time in office was notable because she was the sole female in the legislature for ten of the twelve years that she served, serving as a bridge between the early successes of female candidates in the 1920s and the

---

[42] Senate Daily Journal, Third Extraordinary Session, 28 January 1944, page 37
[43] Assembly Daily Journal, 7 January 1943, page 146

later growth that started in the early 1950s. When Kathryn Niehouse left office in 1954, she had overlapped for one session with Pauline L. Davis, the final 'solo woman' in the legislature. The widow of Assemblyman Lester T. Davis, who died in his sixth year in office, Davis had served as her husband's secretary of years and decided quickly to run for his seat a few months later.

Among her accomplishments was the naming of a lake in Plumas County after her husband and coauthoring the Legislative Open Records Act in 1975. Davis served for nearly 24 years, passing Eleanor Miller to become the longest-serving Assemblywoman in 1972.

A 2018 event organized by Women in California Politics (WICP) brought together women elected to the legislature in from the 1960s-2010s.

Women Who Have Served in Both Houses of the Legislature

Of the 171 women to serve in the legislature in the past century, only forty-six have served in both houses of the legislature. In the 2020 election, Janet Nguyen became to the first to serve in both houses starting in the Senate.

1) *Marian Bergeson*
2) *Lucy Killea*
3) *Teresa P. Hughes*
4) *Cathie Wright*
5) Hilda Solis
6) Deirdre Alpert
7) Betty Karnette
8) Barbara Lee
9) Debra Bowen
10) Martha Escutia
11) Liz Figueroa
12) Deborah Ortiz
13) Jackie Speier
14) *Nell Soto*
15) Sheila James Kuehl
16) Gloria Romero
17) Denise M. Ducheny
18) Elaine Alquist
19) Christine Kehoe
20) Carole Migden
21) Ellen M. Corbett
22) Gloria Negrete-McLeod
23) *Jenny Oropeza*
24) *Pat Wiggins*
25) Loni Hancock
26) Carol Jean Liu
27) Fran Pavley
28) Mimi Walters
29) Lois Wolk
30) Noreen Evans
31) Jean Fuller
32) *Sharon Runner*
33) Cathleen Galgiani
34) Hannah-Beth Jackson
35) Norma J. Torres
36) Holly J. Mitchell
37) **Patricia Bates**
38) **Toni G. Atkins**
39) **Nancy Skinner**
40) Ling Ling Chang
41) **Anna Caballero**
42) **Shannon Grove**
43) **Melissa Melendez**
44) **Susan T. Eggman**
45) **Monique Limon**
46) **Janet Nguyen**

Bold indicates currently serving.   *Italicized* indicates deceased.

A bust of Lt. Governor Mervyn M. Dymally (born in Trinidad), now on the first floor of the State Capitol, was dedicated in 2019.

Foreign Born Legislators

"[O]ne day, my Dad announced that we were going back home to Seoul... just like that - all of my siblings packed up to leave. I wasn't about to go. I wanted to live my own life, to stay and take my chances."
- Assemblywoman Mary Hayashi[44]

Since the earliest days, California's legislators have come from across the globe. As of the start of the 2021-22 session, at least 329 legislators have been born in other nations, not counting the nearly dozen native Californians born here while it was part of other countries[45].

For several years in the early 1870s, the legislature didn't have a single native Californian. In 1871, for example, 101 were born in other states and nineteen were from foreign countries[46].

California state legislators have been born in all 50 states and dozens of nations, kingdoms, and empires. Jack Massion was born in 1888 in what was then the Russian Empire and served in the State Assembly between 1939 and 1946. By the time he was a legislator, the city where he was born was located within the Ukrainian Soviet Socialist Republic. It's interesting to note that the biographies he provided for the California Blue Book while he was in office put his birthplace as "Russia."[47]

Robert Desty[48], born in Quebec in 1827, was elected to the State Senate in 1879. After his election, it was discovered that Desty was not a citizen

---

[44] Far From Home by Mary Chung Hayashi (Tapestry Press; 2003), page 35.
[45] Pedro C. Carrillo, Pablo De la Guerra, Andres Pico, and Mariano G. Vallejo were born in California while it was still part of the Spanish Empire. Vital Emanuel Bangs, Estevan Castro, Manuel A. Castro, Antonio M. De la Guerra, Miriano Malarin, Mariano G. Pacheco, and Romualdo Pacheco were born in California while it was part of the First Mexican Republic.
[46] Legislative Guide... of all the State Officers and Members of the Legislature... by Kean and Dudley (H.S. Crocker and Co.; 1871)
[47] California Blue Book (1942 and 1946 editions)
[48] His full name was Robert Daillebout d'Estimauville de Beaumaucha.

and he wasn't allowed to be sworn into office.[49] Desty immediately returned to New York, where he found that although he had filed a petition to become a citizen in 1849 (and received a certificate recognizing his application), he never formally became a citizen. He claimed to have been naturalized in San Francisco (but the records were destroyed in an 1850 fire) and petitioned to have his citizenship take place retroactively. The petition was denied and Desty became an American citizen in February 1880.

In recent years, Assemblywoman Christy Smith became the first California legislator born in Germany since Frederick Peterson (who served 1933-1936). Smith declined reelection in 2020 to run instead for Congress, so she just missed serving with two other Germany-born legislators, Thurston Smith and Chris Ward, who are just beginning their first terms.

Assemblyman Tyler Diep, elected in 2018, was the first to be born in the Socialist Republic of Vietnam (after the fall of Saigon) while two prior legislators had been born in the Republic of Vietnam while the war was still raging. Diep was defeated in his bid for reelection in the primary by Janet Nguyen and Diedre Thu-Ha Nguyen (both born in the Republic of Vietnam), of whom Janet Nguyen won the General Election.

First elected in 2017, Assemblywoman Wendy Carrillo is the first legislator born in El Salvador, and only the second born in Central American in more than a century. Before the arrival of Norma J. Torres (born in Guatemala) in 2009, it had been 104 years since E. J. Emmons (born in Nicaragua) served in both houses between 1897 and 1905.

The legislature currently has lawmakers born throughout North America, as well as in Europe and Asia. The most recent legislator born in Australia was State Senator Henry McGuinness, who died in office in 1936. The last from Africa was Assemblyman George Ohleyer, born in French Algeria in 1831, who served a single term in 1887. The last legislator from South America was Assemblyman Augustus Daniel Splivalo (of Chile) in 1869.

---

[49] "Desty Not a Citizen" Daily Alta California, 3 February 1880: 1. California Digital Newspaper Collection. Web. Accessed 12 December 2016

Nobody born in Antarctica has yet served in the California state legislature, which appears unlikely to change.

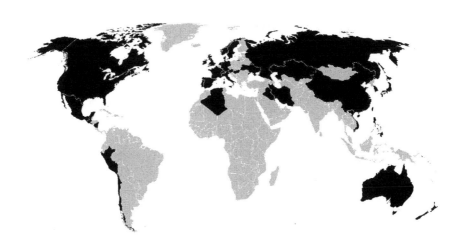

Legislators Born Outside the United States

Algeria (French Algeria)
George Ohleyer

Australia
Frank Graham Finlayson
Joseph W. Jourdan
Leonard M. Landsborough
Henry McGuinness
Timothy O'Connor
Leo H. Susman

Azores (Portugal)
John Garcia Mattos Jr.

Canada
Ronald G. Cameron
Douglas F. Carter

Canada (continued)
Frank R. Devlin
Alexander Gordon
William James Gurnett
Gordon R. Hahn
George Juan Hatfield
William J. Hill
William Arthur Johnstone
Ash Kalra
Martin Knox
William J. Locke
Duncan W. McCallum
John B. McColl
Thomas R. McCormack
Patrick D. McGee
Alex McMillan
J. J. Murphy

Canada (continued)
Edwin Parker
John B. Pelletier
William J. Sinon
Oscar Sutro
A. Van Leuven
Thomas C. West
John N. Young

Canada (New Brunswick Colony, British North America)
S. C. Bugbee
James F. Cunningham
Alfred A. Green
James E. Perley
John Sime

Canada (Newfoundland Province, British North America)
Thomas J. Clunie

Canada (Nova Scotia Colony, British North America)
Thomas Fraser
Alexander Hay
George R. Oulton
Benjamin B. Redding
William Sexton
Henry Starr

Canada (Province of Canada)
John N. Anderson
Charles Dexter Ball
Prescott F. Cogswell
A. D. Duffey
Harry Leander Ells
Peter Wallace Forbes

William H. R. McMartin
H. B. M. Miller
Patrick W. Murphy

Canada (then Province of Lower Canada, British North America)
Carlisle Stewart Abbott
L. I. Hogle
Bernard D. Murphy
Alexander Campbell
Joseph Albert Tivy
Hiram W. Wallis

Chile
Augustus Daniel Splivalo

China (then British Hong Kong)
Edwin Chau

People's Republic of China
Paul Fong
Leland Y. Yee

Denmark
Theodore F. Bagge
Henry Suverkrup

El Salvador
Wendy Carrillo

England
Josiah P. Ames
William H. Ash
John E. Baker
Jabez Banbury
Thomas H. Barber
Robson O. Bell
George H. Burnham

England (continued)
R. C. Carter
J. E. Clark
Charles Clayton
John Crisp Coleman
John A. Cook
Robert Corlett
Frederick Cox
Jacob Croter
John M. Days
Peter Dean
Richard DeLancie
Francis Dunn Jr.
Herbert Johnston Evans
John Fairweather
Robert F. Fisher
William R. George
England (continued)
George B. Godfrey
Charles Goodall
William E. Harper
Josiah W. Haskin
James Haworth
Henry Hawson
Charles Augustus Holland
Thomas Ingram
William Theodore James
Robert S. Johnson
John P. Jones
Frederick William Lambourn
Montague Richard Leverson
Aubrey M. Lumley
A. C. McAlister
Geoffrey F. Morgan
Walter Murray
Bertram Schlesinger
Josiah Sims
Herbert W. Slater

John J. Smith
William J. Sweasey
Henry Thompson
Edward Humphrey Tickle
John Roland Tyrrell
James H. Warwick
John White
David Caledffrwd Williams
Edward I. Wolfe
Michael Wornum
George A. Young

France
Jim Cooper
Jose Maria Covarrubias
Emile A. Gaussail
Frederick Lux
Joseph Routier

Germany
Charles Jost
Adam Rhiel
Adolphus G. Russ
John Seibe
John D. Siebe
Christy Smith
Thurston Smith
John Staude
Chris Ward
Christian Wentz
Herman Wohler

**Germany
(Duchy of Brunswick)**
Frederick Augustus Hihn

**Germany
(German Confederation)**
Frederick G. Raisch
Herman Rankin

Germany (German Empire)
Frederick Peterson
H. W. A. Weske

**Germany
(Grand Duchy of Baden)**
Julius Kahn
Mel Vogel

**Germany
(Kingdom of Bavaria)**
Frederick C. Franck
Leonard J. Rose

**Germany
(Kingdom of Hanover)**
William Barklage
Martin Lammers

Germany (Kingdom of Prussia)
Robert J. Betge
Samuel Braunhart
B. S. Broderson
Max Brooks
Rudolph Klotz
Otto Mentzell
Paul Neuman
Fred G. E. Tittel

Germany (Kingdom of Saxony)
Charles G. Hubner

**Denmark
(North German Confederation)**
Wilhelm Asmussen
Hans Christian Nelson

Germany (Principality of Reuss)
William E. Eichelroth

Guatemala
Norma J. Torres

Hungary
Agostan Haraszthy
Ernest L. Konnyu

Iran
Adrin Nazarian

Iraq
Wadie P. Deddeh

Ireland
Thomas Beck
Robert Bell
John S. Boyston
William Broderick
John Burns
Michael J. Burns
James Dwyer Byrnes
William Caldwell
George Jerome Campbell
Thompson Campbell
Matthew Canavan
Patrick Canney
James Gilmore Carson
John Conness
James E. Connolly
Patrick Connolly

Ireland (continued)

Bernard Conway
William Cronan
John R. Cronin
John M. Crowell
Samuel T. Curtis
Peter Deveny
James Dixon
M. J. Donovan
John T. Dougherty
John G. Downey
James A. Duffy
David Dwyer
Daniel Ferguson
William K. Forsyth
Thomas Fowler
Patrick Tracy Gaffey
Dennis Geary
Charles Gildea
Joseph C. Gorman
John Hamill
Thomas Hansbrow
Marcus Sparks Harloe Sr.
Lawrence J. Hoey
Alexander Hunter
James Hynes
Thomas Kane
John W. Keegan
Martin Kelly
John O'Brien Kennedy
William P. Kennedy
Edward Lawlor
Michael Lane
Thomas J. Lenehan
Robert Ludgate
Frank Mahon
David Mahoney
James J. McBride

John Wallace McBride
John J. McCallion
Michael McCarthy
T. W. McColliam
Frank McCoppin
James McCoy
James McCudden
John Weir McDonald
Patrick McHale
Thomas McInery
John McKeon
Michael Meagher
Anthony James Meany
Thomas Francis Mitchell
Patrick Mundy
John Malachi Murphy
James C. Nealon
John G. Noonan
Edward Nunan
William O'Connell
Miles P. O'Connor
Jasper O'Farrell
Florence J. O'Neill
Patrick. Plover
Thomas Renison
Philip A. Roach
James M. Roane
Pierce Howard Ryan
William H. Savage
Edward Smyth
Edward Fallis Spence
Robert Stewart
D. C. Sullivan
John J. Tobin
Hugh Toner
Timothy Edward Treacy
James H. Watson
John P. West

Isle of Man, British Crown Dependency
Philip Caine

Italy (Grand Duchy of Tuscany)
Egisto C. Palmieri

Italy (Kingdom of Italy)
Marcino G. Del Mutolo

Lebanon
Khatchik "Katcho" Achadjian

Mexico
Marco A. Firebaugh
Patty Lopez
Pedro Nava
Blanca Rubio
Susan Rubio
Jose Solorio

Mexico (Viceroyalty of New Spain, Spanish Empire)
Ygnacio Del Valle

Netherlands
Fred W. Chel
John M. W. Moorlach

New Zealand
Leo T. McCarthy
Montague Bryant Steadman

Nicaragua
E. J. Emmons

Northern Ireland
James McDonnell Jr.
Joseph McKeown

Norway
Maurice K. Johannessen
Thorwald K. Nelson

Nova Scotia
John Frazier
Thomas O'Brien

Peru
Manuel Torres

Philippines
Rob Bonta

Republic of China (Taiwan)
Susan Bonilla
Ling Ling Chang
Kansen Chu
Ted Lieu

Scotland
John Borland
John C. Bradley
Archibald E. Brock
Robert Chalmers
Charles D. Douglas
John Gardner
C. W. Kingsley
F. A. McDougall
William McMann
Thomas Mein

Scotland (continued)
Richard Melrose
William Boyd Parker
John A. Watson
John Yule

South Korea
Steven S. Choi
Mary Hayashi
Young Kim

Sweden
W. H. Carlson
Hjalmar E. Holmquist
Adam L. C. Hjalmar Kylberg

Switzerland
Paul F. Fratessa
Henry Alphonse Pellet
Charles Wolleb
Trinidad (British West Indies)
Mervyn M. Dymally

Ukraine (then Russian Empire)
Jack Massion

U.S. Virgin Islands (then Danish West Indies of the Dano-Norwegian Realm)
William Alexander Conn

Vietnam (Republic of Vietnam)
Janet Nguyen
Van Tran

Vietnam (Socialist Republic of Vietnam)
Tyler Diep

"Born At Sea"
John Rogers Cook

California's Youngest Legislators (1921-2021)[50]

	House	Legislator	Assumed Office Age	Year
1	Assembly	Maurice E. Atkinson	23.6	1939
2	Assembly	Hugh R. Pomeroy	23.6	1923
3	Assembly	Augustus F. Jewett Jr.	23.7	1927
4	Assembly	Sam M. Greene	24.4	1931
5	Assembly	William F. Knowland	24.5	1933
6	**Assembly**	**Alex T. Lee**	**25.4**	**2020**
7	Assembly	William B. Hornblower	26	1921
8	Assembly	Tom Hunter Louttit	26.1	1925
9	Assembly	John R. Lewis	26.1	1980
10	Assembly	Frederick F. Houser	26.1	1931
11	Assembly	Albert F. Ross Jr.	26.2	1921
12	Assembly	Sebastian Ridley-Thomas	26.3	2013
13	Assembly	Tom McClintock	26.4	1982
14	Assembly	Thomas H. Kuchel	26.4	1937
15	Assembly	E. Walton Hedges Jr.	26.4	1927
16	Assembly	Edwin A. Mueller	26.6	1923
17	Assembly	Jim Costa	26.7	1978
18	Assembly	B. J. Feigenbaum	26.7	1927
19	Senate	John F. McCarthy	26.9	1951
20	Assembly	C. Ray Robinson	26.9	1931
21	Assembly	Walter J. Schmidt	~27	1921
22	Assembly	Franklin Heck	~27	1921
23	Assembly	Ian C. Calderon	27.1	2012
24	Assembly	George W. Rochester	27.3	1927
25	Assembly	Augustus F. Hawkins	27.3	1935

Bold indicates currently serving. *Italicized* indicates deceased.

---

[50] Only includes legislators for whom a full birthdate (rather than just a birth year) is known.

Youngest Legislators

"I was the "baby" of the legislature, youngest member in years as in tenure, but here, too, I saw that Hollywood had a connotation that drew attention to me aside from everything else, and it was not always indulgent attention."
- Assemblyman Milton M. Golden[51]

The 2021-22 Session arrived with freshman Assemblyman Alex T. Lee, the first state legislator born in the 1990s. At just 25 years old when he assumed office, Lee is the youngest legislator since Maurice E. Atkinson joined the Assembly at age 23 in 1939. Prior to Atkinson, the last legislator younger than Lee was Assemblyman William F. Knowland (24 years old in 1933) who had a meteoric rise which led him to the U.S. Senate at 37. He would become Senate Majority Leader and, as the title of his biography suggests, end up One Step from the White House[52].

Looking at the legislators who assumed office in the past five decades, those first elected in their 20s served the longest (an average of 10.3 years), the second longest-serving were legislators elected in their 50s (serving 8.12 years), with those arriving in their 30s and 40s serving about six months less.

Arriving early isn't everything. Lord Charles Snowden Fairfax (the 10th Baron of Cameron) was a nobleman from birth and had a bright future ahead of him. He was elected to the Assembly at 23 and became Assembly Speaker at 24. He was elected to statewide office at age 27 and would have been a strong candidate for ever higher office until he was stabbed in the chest by a fellow Assemblyman shortly after his 30th birthday.

---

[51] Hollywood Lawyer (Signet Books; 1960), page 74.
[52] Definitely put One Step from the White House: The Rise and Fall of William F. Knowland by Gayle Montgomery, James W. Johnson and Paul Manolis (University of California Press; 1998) on your reading list.

California's Oldest Legislators (1921-2021)[53]

	House	Legislator	Leaving Office Age	Year
1	Senate	Ralph C. Dills	88.8	1998
2	Assembly	Albert I. Stewart	88.5	1958
3	Senate	Alfred E. Alquist	88.3	1996
4	Assembly	Mervyn M. Dymally	82.6	2008
5	Assembly	Nell Soto	82.4	2008
6	Senate	Frank L. Gordon	82	1948
7	Senate	Charles King	81.4	1936
8	Senate	Leroy F. Greene	80.8	1998
9	Senate	Herschel Rosenthal	80.7	1998
10	Senate	Cadet Taylor	80.3	1928
11	Senate	Nathan F. Coombs	80	1960
12	Senate	Bob Margett	79.6	2008
13	Senate	Charles H. Deuel	79.4	1947
14	Assembly	Tom Bane	78.9	1992
15	Assembly	Samuel L. Heisinger	78.8	1949
16	Senate	Charles Brown	78.7	1962
17	Senate	Harry L. Parkman	77.9	1956
18	Senate	J. I. Wagy	77.9	1942
19	Senate	Arthur W. Way	77.8	1956
20	Assembly	Thomas J. Doyle	77.6	1957
21	Senate	William A. Craven	77.4	1998
22	Assembly	Montivel A. Burke	77.4	1962
23	Assembly	Betty Karnette	77.2	2008
24	Senate	Clyde A. Watson	77.2	1952
25	Assembly	Frank D. Lanterman	77.1	1978

Italicized indicates deceased.

---

[53] Because this is a list based on legislator age when they left office, only former legislators appear on this list.

Oldest Legislators

In the past few sessions, the legislature has added some of its oldest freshmen in decades. In 2016, Assemblyman Steven S. Choi was sworn into his first term at nearly 73 years old, making him the oldest freshman legislator since Assemblyman Albert I. Stewart arrived in 1945. Two years later, that record was broken.

In the early sessions of the 1850s-1860s, even the older members of the legislature weren't of an age that we today would consider particularly advanced. A major driver of the legislators' low ages was the large number of young men coming to California for mining jobs in the first decades after statehood.

The voyage to California was difficult (either crossing the Plains in a covered wagon, hiking across Panama, or sailing rounding Tierra del Fuego) and frequently unappealing to older and more established residents of the eastern states. As a result, the legislators elected in the early years tended to be exceptionally young. In the 16th Session of the Legislature (1866), the youngest Assemblyman was John W. Satterwhite at age 24, while A. J. Huestis was the oldest at 49.

The oldest known freshman legislator was Assemblyman Anthony Jennings Bledsoe, born in 1808, who joined the legislature at 83 years old in 1891. Bledsoe served for nearly six years before leaving office in 1896.

Assemblywoman Nell Soto was the oldest woman to ever serve in the legislature, leaving office at 82 years old, although she will be surpassed by Senator Bates during the current session.

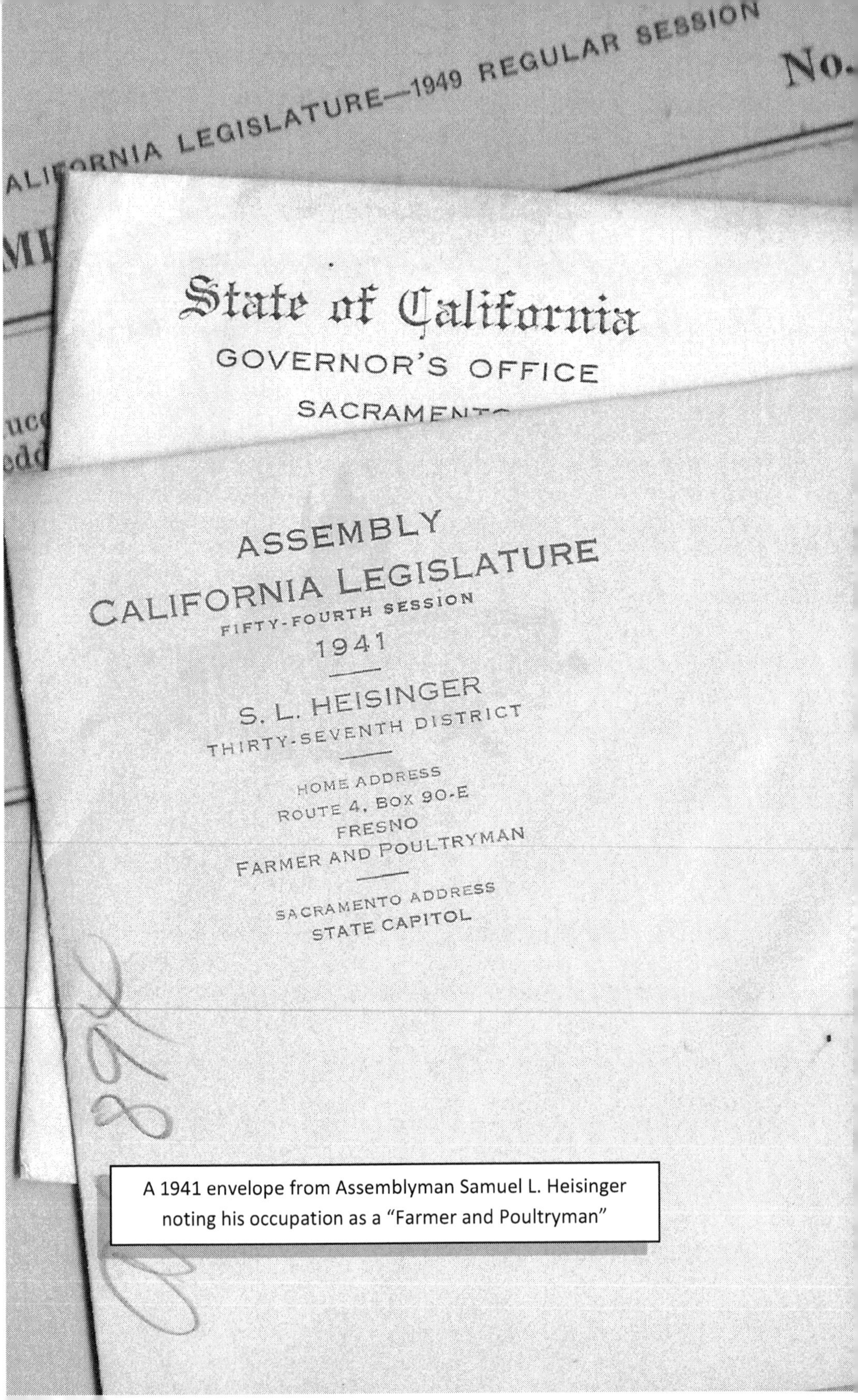

State of California

GOVERNOR'S OFFICE

SACRAMENTO

ASSEMBLY
CALIFORNIA LEGISLATURE
FIFTY-FOURTH SESSION
1941

—

S. L. HEISINGER
THIRTY-SEVENTH DISTRICT

—

HOME ADDRESS
ROUTE 4, BOX 90-E
FRESNO
FARMER AND POULTRYMAN

—

SACRAMENTO ADDRESS
STATE CAPITOL

A 1941 envelope from Assemblyman Samuel L. Heisinger
noting his occupation as a "Farmer and Poultryman"

Occupations

> "Until 1967, members had just one Capitol secretary, only during session, and one district office secretary fulltime, plus district office rent and a $150 per month stipend... Assemblyman Alan Pattee (R-Monterey), a Harvard grad and successful dairyman, used his $150 per month stipend to pay his milker, proclaiming "I have a phone in the barn.""
> - Assemblyman Bill Bagley[54]

The members of the legislature have included a large number of attorneys, judges, teachers and professors, surveyors, lumbermen, ranchers and cattlemen, but also pilots, vintners, police officers and U.S. Marshalls, sheriffs and district attorneys, newspaper editors and publishers, surgeons, miners, military officers, machinists and plumbers, almond growers and a rice farmer, a child psychologist, and at least one "house painter".

A few of the more unusual occupations have included "wholesale liquor merchant" (Assemblyman Charles M. Fisher) and "wholesale cigar merchant" (Senator John P. Hare). Nathan Gilmore (who served as an Assemblyman in 1874) was a breeder of Angora goats, while Danny Gilmore (who served in the Assembly during the 2009-10 session) was a thirty-year Highway Patrol officer. One of the more notable was Assemblyman Benjamin F. Moore, who listed his occupation as "Gentleman of Elegant Leisure" when he signed in as a delegate to the 1849 constitutional convention.

Of all the occupations that legislators have had, one that stands out is that of John B. Pelletier; none. Prior to his election in 1934, Pelletier was unemployed and homeless, working at a campaign headquarters in exchange for the meals they provided to the 'volunteers'. A 2010 Capitol Weekly article described his election as "Artie [Samish] found a homeless man named John Pelletier, put him in a suit, and ran him for office. He won handily and served 10 years in the Assembly." While not inaccurate,

---

[54] California's Golden Years (IGS Press; 2009), page 7.

this description does neglect that Pelletier was well-educated economist and attorney who had graduated from private liberal arts Bates College in Maine and studied law at Boston University.

One interesting thing that happened about a century ago was the inclusion, in each session's Final History, of the occupations of each of the members of the State Assembly. Not immediately adopting the practice, the Senate began the practice about twenty years later.

It's worth noting that this information was self-reported by each legislator and occasionally their responses varied over time. In 1939, his first year as a legislator, Ralph Dills listed his occupation as teacher while by 1947, his last full session in the Assembly, Dills listed himself as an attorney. By 1998, when Dills finally retired from the Senate after 32 years there, he reported his occupation as a "full-time legislator."

Among the more novel occupations of California lawmakers were "ballplayer," listed by former Philadelphia Athletics catcher James Joseph Byrnes who served in the Assembly in 1915, "undertaker" by Assemblyman Mark A. Pierce in 1925, and Assemblyman H. J. Widenmann who identified as a beer brewer.

In early years, when the legislature met for only a few months every other year, legislators listed only their outside professions. For example, in 1925 the Assembly was composed of twenty-six attorneys, five farmers, four ranchers, two housewives, three publishers, a lumberman, and a railroad conductor (among others).

In 1945, Assemblyman Albert Dekker became the first lawmaker to provide his legislative employment as his profession - his actual career was as an actor who appeared in 75 films including *Experiment Perilous* (1944) and *Middle of the Night* (1959).

The trend grew, and today a majority of lawmakers are following in the footsteps of Dekker.

Other Offices

"I wasn't in Congress long enough to leave a legacy that comes anywhere near qualifying me for statesmanship, but for the time God and the voters gave me to serve there, I did my best to apply an honorable standard."
- Assemblyman James E. Rogan[55]

California's legislators have gone on to hold a wide range of other offices. Within California state government, well over a hundred have been elected to constitutional office, including fifteen who became Governor of California[56] and four others who served as Governor elsewhere. At least 177 state legislators have been sent to Congress, including twelve who represented other states or territories[57].

In terms of holding elected offices, there will almost certainly never be another legislator like Thomas Jefferson Green. He started his political career in his home state of North Carolina, where he became a member of the state legislature. He quickly moved to Florida, where he became a member of that territorial legislature. He left Florida to serve as a General in the Volunteer Army during the Texas Revolution *(keep in mind that he was only 33 years old).*

The war ended with Texas as an independent nation and Green was promptly elected as a Representative to the Republic of Texas Congress. After serving there and then in the Texian Militia, he moved to California where he served in the U.S. Army during the Occupation of California. In

---

[55] Rough Edges: My Unlikely Road from Welfare to Washington (HarperCollins; 2004), page 307.

[56] Six governors served only in the Senate (Bartlett, Booth, Gillett, Olson, Pacheco and Perkins), while six others served only in the Assembly (Bigler, Davis, Downey, Johnson, Wilson and Young). Three others (Deukmejian, Irwin and Merriam) served in both.

[57] Two of the eleven served as U.S. Senators from other states; Senator John P. Jones of Nevada and Alexander O. Anderson of Tennessee.

1849, Green was elected to his fourth legislature, becoming one of California's first State Senators.

The first session of California's legislature actually got its nickname ("Legislature of a Thousand Drinks") from Green. In an attempt to convince his colleagues to elect him as one of California's first U.S. Senators, Green frequently called for temporary recesses to take legislators to a local bar for a round of drinks[58]. Perhaps fortunately for the lasting reputation of the new state, Green was unsuccessful and John C. Fremont and William M. Gwin became our first U.S. Senators.

Twenty-six legislators have been Lieutenant Governors (23 for California and one each for Iowa, Missouri and Nevada) and twenty became Secretary of State (17 in California, and three others in Nevada, Oregon, Vermont, and Wisconsin[59]. The record in Executive Branch service by a legislator is held by State Senator Romualdo Pacheco and Assemblyman Gray Davis, who each held three constitutional offices (including both serving as Governor).

Assemblyman Paul Peek had an interesting tour of the three branches of government. Peek started in the legislative branch, serving as Assembly Speaker in 1939. He next moved to the executive branch, being appointed Secretary of State in 1940 and serving until 1942. Finally, he finished as a California Supreme Court justice from 1962 to 1966. A similarly unique case of a person interacting with the law from every angle can be found with William T. Wallace. Wallace enforced the law as Attorney General from 1856 to 1858, interpreted the law as Chief Justice of the California Supreme Court from 1872 to 1879, and ended his career writing laws as an Assemblyman in 1885.

California legislators have also held high federal offices. Assemblyman Stephen J. Field served in the second session during 1851. He became an Associate Justice of the California Supreme Court from 1857 to 1859 and

---

[58] See History of California, Volume 23 by Hubert Howe Bancroft (History Company, 1888) for more information about the Green and his drinks.

[59] James McMillan Shafter, California's Senate President pro Tem in 1862, also served in two other state legislatures (including as Speaker of the Wisconsin State Assembly in 1851) and as Secretary of State in Vermont and Wisconsin.

was elevated to Chief Justice in 1859[60]. Field served as Chief Justice until 1863, when President Abraham Lincoln appointed him to the U.S. Supreme Court. By the time he retired in 1899, Field had become the longest-serving U.S. Supreme Court Justice[61].

California legislators have served the nation as ambassadors, military generals, Secretary of Defense (Caspar Weinberger), Attorney General (Joseph McKenna), Senate Majority Leader (William F. Knowland), and the currently-serving House Majority Leader (Kevin McCarthy)[62].

One federal job that no modern legislators seems to be clamoring for these days is the one held by Assemblyman Fred Hugo Hartmann in 1900. According to his biography in a state publication, "during the bubonic plague investigation in San Francisco, [Hartmann] was official disinfector for the United States Health Commission."[63]

Federal Offices

Stephen J. Field	Supreme Court Associate Justice (1863-1897)
Joseph McKenna	Attorney General (1897-1898)
Joseph McKenna	Supreme Court Associate Justice (1898-1925)
William F. Knowland	Senate Majority Leader (1953-1955)
Caspar Weinberger	Secretary of Health, Education and Welfare (1973-1975)
Caspar Weinberger	Secretary of Defense (1981-1987)
Louis Caldera	Secretary of the Army (1998-2001)
Hilda Solis	Secretary of Labor (2009-2013)
Xavier Becerra	Secretary of Health and Human Services (Nominee)

---

[60] Field was elevated to California Chief Justice after the previous Chief Justice killed U.S. Senator David Broderick in a duel and fled the state.

[61] Field's remained the longest serving Supreme Court Justice until William O. Douglas broke his record in 1973.

[62] None of the six highest-ranking Californians to serve in the federal government (Ronald Reagan, Richard Nixon, Herbert Hoover, Kamala Harris, Nancy Pelosi and Earl Warren) ever served as state legislators.

[63] 1907 California Blue Book (California State Printer; 1907), page 396.

Other States and Territories

Lewis R. Bradley	Governor of Nevada
Willis W. Bradley	Naval Governor of Guam
James W. Denver	Governor of Kansas Territory
Lilburn W. Boggs	Governor of Missouri
Andres Pico	Governor of Alta California (Mexico)
Charles Robinson	Governor of Kansas Territory
	Governor of Kansas
Thomas Baker	Lieutenant Governor of Iowa
Lilburn W. Boggs	Lieutenant Governor of Missouri
James S. Slingerland	Lieutenant Governor of Nevada
Jasper Babcock	Secretary of State of Nevada
Thompson Campbell	Secretary of State of Illinois
Edward Fallis Spence	State Treasurer of Nevada
Alexander O. Anderson	U.S. Senator from Tennessee
John P. Jones	U.S. Senator from Nevada
Delos R. Ashley	U.S. Representative from Nevada
Thomas Fitch	U.S. Representative from Nevada
Thomas J. Henley	U.S. Representative from Indiana
C. W. Kendall	U.S. Representative from Nevada
Lansing Stout	U.S. Representative from Oregon
Nelson Taylor	U.S. Representative from New York
Henry Worthington[64]	U.S. Representative from Nevada
Selucius Garfielde	Delegate from Washington Territory
Samuel A. Merritt	Delegate from Idaho Territory

---

[64] Worthington, the first U.S. Representative from Nevada after statehood, was a pallbearer at the funeral of President Abraham Lincoln.

Other States and Territories (continued)

C. G. W. French	Chief Justice, Arizona Supreme Court
Samuel A. Merritt	Chief Justice, Utah Territory Supreme Court
James A. Banks	House Speaker, Nevada Territory
Elwood T. Beatty	Council President, Idaho Territory
	House Speaker, Idaho Territory
R. D. Ferguson	House Speaker, Nevada Territory
Henry A. Gaston	House Speaker, Nevada Territory
Miles N. Mitchell	House Speaker, Nevada Territory
H. G. Parker	Senate President pro Tem, Nevada
James M. Shafter	House Speaker, Wisconsin
James S. Slingerland	Senate President pro Tem, Nevada
Ninian E. Whiteside	House Speaker, Wisconsin

Other Nations

Charles Duncombe	Member, Legislative Assembly of Upper Canada *British North America*
Parker H. French[65]	Minister of Hacienda (Secretary of the Treasury) *Republic of Nicaragua*
	Minister Plenipotentiary and Envoy Extraordinary *Republic of Nicaragua*
Edward J. C. Kewan	Judge Advocate General *Republic of Nicaragua*
Mariano G. Vallejo	Member, Territorial Legislature of Alta California *First Mexican Republic*
	Delegate, Mexican Congress *(Did Not Attend)* *First Mexican Republic*

---

[65] Kentucky Barracuda by Joe Goodbody (Mascot Books; 2018)

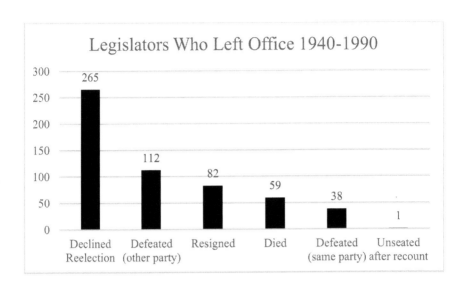

Legislators Who Left Office 1940-1990

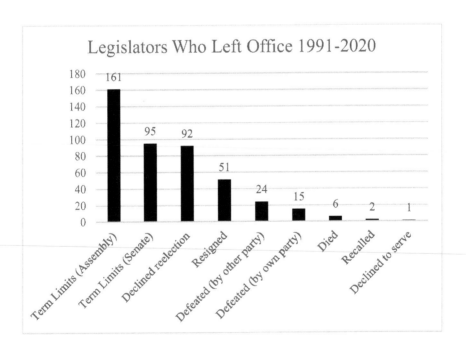

Legislators Who Left Office 1991-2020

Leaving Office

> **"As I conclude my legislative duties in Sacramento and depart for the nation's Capitol in Washington, D.C. to be sworn in as the first woman to represent the people of the 37th Congressional District, I leave with a sense of accomplishment and fond memories of my four years of service in the California State Legislature."**
> - *Assemblywoman Juanita Millender-McDonald*[66]

In recent years, the primary reasons that legislators have left office have been either term limits preventing the seeking of additional terms or the desire to move on to other opportunities because of the pressures created by term limits. For example, after seventy years of seeing an average of two lawmakers per decade leaving office to seek or take a seat on a county board of supervisors, the past decade has seen four departures (of whom, only Holly Mitchell was successful).

1940-1990

During the fifty years between the start of WWII and the start of the first term limits (1940 and 1990), a total of 557 legislators left office. A large number simply refused to run again, either to retire or to seek another office outside of the legislature. The second largest group was lawmakers who left office after being defeated by a member of another political party.

Of the least common reasons to leave the legislature, we find two declined reelection to study religion (in 1976 and 1990), two who left to enter military service (in 1941 and 1944), and one who announced that he was leaving to study poetry (in 1966). Charles B. Garrigus, who left to pursue poetry, served as Poet Laureate for California for the next thirty-four years.

---

[66] "Letter of Departure," <u>Assembly Daily Journal</u>, 13 May 1996.

Legislators Who Termed Out of Both Houses

2002	Bill Leonard		
2004	Deirdre Alpert Byron Sher	Jim Brulte John Vasconcellos	John L. Burton
2006	Debra Bowen Tim Leslie	Martha Escutia Bill Morrow	Ray Haynes Jackie Speier
2008	Dick Ackerman Sheila J. Kuehl	Jim Battin Mike Machado Tom McClintock	Betty Karnette Bob Margett
2010	Roy Ashburn Tom Torlakson	Denise M. Ducheny	George Runner[67]
2012	Elaine Alquist Tom Harman	Charles Calderon Alan Lowenthal	Gilbert Cedillo
2014	Wes Chesbro Darrell Steinberg	Ellen M. Corbett Mark Wyland	Lou Correa
2016	Loni Hancock Fran Pavley	Mark Leno Lois Wolk	Carol Liu
2020	Jim Beall	Cathleen Galgiani	Hannah-Beth Jackson
2022	Patricia Bates	Robert Hertzberg	
2024	Toni G. Atkins Nancy Skinner	Steven Bradford	Anthony Portantino
2026	Anna Caballero Tom Umberg	Shannon Grove	Brian Jones
2028	John Laird		

---

[67] Although he was elected to a term that ended in 2012, Runner left office in 2010 to take a seat on the Board of Equalization.

Assemblyman Franklin J. Potter, one of the two who left for military service, eventually headed the legal division for the Office of Military Government for Hesse at the time of "Operation Bodysnatch", when the U.S. military recovered the bodies of King Frederick Wilhelm I, Frederick the Great, and Field Marshall Paul von Hindenburg which had been stolen from their tombs by Nazis in the final days of the war.

1991-2020

Term limits in California were created when voters approved Proposition 140 in 1990. Under the law, members were limited to three 2-year terms in the State Assembly and two 4-year terms in the Senate. Although weakened slightly by a court challenge[68], the original term limits law remained in effect for 22 years.

A total of 432 legislators served during the first term limits era. Of these term limits era legislators, a quarter (109) began their service prior to term limits[69], one third each arrived during the 1990s and 2000s, and 32 were elected in the 2010s before the new term limits law passed.

One common misunderstanding about term limits that I feel obligated to correct is that it significantly increased the number of new legislators arriving in Sacramento[70]. It did not. What it did was make the turnover happen at a much more uniform rate, removing members who had served for decades. The loss of these longest-serving members quickly dropped the prior legislative experience of the entire house.

---

[68] The decision permitted legislators who were elected in Special Elections and served less than half of a term to not have that partial term count towards their term limits totals.

[69] These legislators included three first elected in the 1950s, 11 first elected in the 1960s, 38 first elected in the 1970s, and 56 first elected in the 1980s. The two outliers were Senator Ralph Dills (first elected in 1939) and Assemblyman Sal Cannella, the last pre-term limits legislator, who was elected in a 1990 special election months before the law passed.

[70] The legislature saw 147 new members in the 1990s and 145 in the 2000s. This wasn't actually that far from the average of 151 new members per decade that the legislature averaged between previous seven decades.

A major change that term limits did bring was accelerating the arrival of women. Between 1918 and 1989, only 38 women were elected to the legislature. During that same period, 925 men were elected to first terms. By comparison, women made up about one in five new legislators elected under the original term limits law.

Of the 432 members to serve in the first term limits era, 185 termed out of the Assembly only, 77 termed out of the Senate only and 43 termed out of both houses (127 never termed out of either house).

Tom Harman was the legislator who termed out fastest. Because of the timing of a special election, he left office after 12 years (5.5 years in the Assembly and 6.5 years in the Senate). A more advantageously scheduled special election gave Tim Leslie the longest tenure before terming out, with 16 years of term limits era service (9.5 years in the Senate and 6.5 years in the Assembly).

There are only nine members who are currently on track to term out of a second house. These nine are currently Senators who have already termed out of the Assembly.

New Term Limits

In 2012, voters brought three major changes to California Legislature; new term limits, the top two primary, and the largest freshman class that the Assembly had seen in a generation.

The passage of Proposition 28 (2012) brought new rules; members could serve up to 12 years in either house[71]. As of the 2016 General Election, 101 members have been elected in the new term limits era. New term limits legislators have, on average, been slightly older than their predecessors[72].

---

[71] One interesting impact was that because the unit of measure in the new term limits law was years (instead of terms) the cap of 12 years wasn't impacted by special elections partial terms.

[72] The average age of legislators elected under new term limits is 46.9 compared to 45.5 during original term limits.

Resignations (2005-2020)

As crazy as it sounds, the first person to ever resign from the California state legislature did so a full nine months before the federal government approved statehood. On December 21, 1849, William C. Van Voorhies resigned from the State Assembly in order to become our first civilian Secretary of State[73].

> *Hall of Assembly*
> *San Jose, Dec. 21st 1849*
>
> *To the Hon. T. J. White, Speaker,*
>
> *Sir,*
> *Having concluded to accept an appointment with which the Executive of the State, by and with the advice and consent of the Senate, has honored me; I hereby respectfully tender my resignation as a Representative from the District of San Francisco to take affect [sp.] immediately.*
> *With sentiments of high consideration*
> *I have the honor to be your servant,*
> *Very Respectfully,*
>
> W. VAN VOORHIES

In his letter, Assemblymember Van Voorhies balances the formality of the notification of his resignation with a reflection on the honor of his recent appointment.

As you read the resignation letters on the following pages, you'll notice that some are abbreviated formal notices with little personal touch,

---

[73] Henry Halleck, a military officer who would later serve as General-in-Chief of the Union armies during the Civil War, had served as the military secretary of state during the occupation of California and was a delegate to the 1849 constitutional convention held in Monterey.

while others will proudly expand on the accomplishments that the legislator was most proud of. You'll also notice differences in tone, with some sounding like a mournful goodbye while others make no attempt to conceal a burning anger.

In all cases, these letters were taken directly from the Daily Journals of the two houses with only minor formatting changes for consistency. Please note; the word count is starts with the salutation and ends with the closing, but does not include the heading (date and address block) or signature.

2020

State Senator Holly J. Mitchell (SD-30) resigned on December 6 after being elected to the Los Angeles County Board of Supervisors. Her resignation letter was 147 words[74].

December 6, 2020
The Honorable Toni G. Atkins
President pro Tempore of the Senate

Dear President pro Tempore Atkins: In November 2020, I was elected to the Board of Supervisors for Los Angeles County. Today, I offer my resignation from the Senate upon taking my oath of office for Los Angeles County on Sunday, December 6, 2020.

I would like to thank the men and women of the California State Senate for affording me the honor and opportunity to serve the great people of this state. The one million of us who call the 30th Senate District home are truly blessed to have neighbors that reflect the diversity of the world.

---

[74] Senate Daily Journal. 7 December 2020, page 13.

It has been my pleasure to serve 10 years in the California State Legislature, carrying 118 bills and authoring 90 state laws that aimed to create a California in which ALL children thrive.

I came, I learned, I fought for justice. Now . . . I'm out!!
(Mic drop!)
Sincerely,

HOLLY J. MITCHELL
Senator, 30th District

Assemblymember Melissa Melendez (AD-67) resigned on May 18 after being elected to the State Senate. Her resignation letter was 59 words[75].

May 15, 2020

The Honorable Anthony Rendon
Speaker of the Assembly
State Capitol, Room 219
Sacramento, California

Dear Mr. Speaker: As a result of my election to the unexpired term of office for the 28th State Senatorial District, I am hereby and respectfully submitting my resignation as State Assemblymember of the 67th State

Assembly District. My resignation is effective upon taking the oath of office for the 28th State Senate District on May 18, 2020.
Respectfully,

MELISSA A. MELENDEZ, Assembly Member
Sixty-seventh District

---

[75] Assembly Daily Journal. 18 May 2020, page 4557

2019

State Senator Jeff Stone (SD-28). Prior to Stone, the last State Senator to resign in order to accept a non-judiciary federal appointment was William E. Coombs, who resigned in 1973 to work for Assistant Treasury Secretary Edward L. Morgan. His resignation letter was 59 words[76].

October 31, 2019

The Honorable Toni G. Atkins
President pro Tempore of the Senate

Dear Senator Atkins: I would like to take this opportunity to inform you that I will resign my position as a California State Senator upon taking the oath of office as the Western Regional Director for the United States Department of Labor on November 1, 2019.

It has been an honor serving the State of California, and I look forward to working with you in the future in my new position.
Sincerely,

JEFF STONE
Senator, 28th District

Assemblymember Brian D. Dahle (AD-01) resigned on June 12 after being elected to the State Senate. His resignation letter was 54 words[77].

June 11, 2019

The Honorable Anthony Rendon
Speaker of the Assembly
State Capitol, Room 219
Sacramento, California

---

[76] Senate Daily Journal. 31 October 2019, page 3010.
[77] Assembly Daily Journal. 12 June 2019, page 2257

Dear Mr. Speaker: As a result of my election to the unexpired term of office for the 1st Senatorial District, I respectfully submit my resignation as State Assembly Member for the 1st Assembly District.

My resignation is effective upon taking the oath of office for the 1st Senate District on June 12, 2019.
Sincerely,

BRIAN DAHLE

State Senator Ted Gaines (SD-01) resigned on January 8 to become a member of the State Board of Equalization. His resignation letter was 70 words[78].

January 8, 2019

The Honorable Toni G. Atkins
President pro Tempore of the Senate

Dear President pro Tempore Atkins: It has been an honor to represent and serve the constituents of the First Senate District for the last seven years.

I will be grateful to represent the people of the Board of Equalization's First District. However, I will be saddened to resign from the State Senate upon taking the oath of office for the Board of Equalization. Respectfully,

TED GAINES
Senator, 1st District

---

[78] Senate Daily Journal. 8 January 2019, page 54.

State Senator Ricardo Lara (SD-33) resigned on January 7 to become Insurance Commissioner. His resignation letter was 303 words[79].

January 4, 2019

The Honorable Toni G. Atkins
President pro Tempore of the Senate

Dear President pro Tempore Atkins: In November 2018, I was elected California Insurance Commissioner. Today, I offer my resignation from the Senate upon taking the oath of office for Insurance Commissioner.

It has been my greatest honor and privilege to serve the constituents of the 33rd Senate District and the people of California. This transition is the culmination of nearly 20 years of service in the Legislature as a staffer, Assembly Member, and now as a Senator. The Legislature has empowered women and working families, fought for equity and justice, expanded access to healthcare, and created a state that is both an environmental and economic leader. Only in this great country, and this great state, could the son of immigrants become a State Senator, and now the 8th California Insurance Commissioner.

I have watched our Legislature grow more diverse and inclusive. As a member of the nation's largest LGBTQ Legislative Caucus I have helped our state move toward equality for all. I have been part of many "firsts," including voting for our first Latino President pro Tempore in more than a century and our first woman and LGBTQ President pro Tempore in California's history. I will always be proud of my part in helping to align our constitutional values with our legislative vision of working on behalf of all Californians.

California is the country's moral compass, and I thank my colleagues in the Senate and Assembly for your bold leadership. I will miss you and the staff that make the Legislature a special place. I leave with a heavy heart but knowing that the future of our state is in good hands. I look forward in my new role to continuing to work alongside our great

---

[79] Senate Daily Journal. 7 January 2019, page 42.

Senate and Assembly and constitutional leaders to promote a fair and equitable state that serves everyone.
Sincerely,

RICARDO LARA
Senator, 33rd District

2018

State Senator Tony Mendoza (SD-32) resigned on February 22 as the Senate was preparing to consider Senate Resolution 85 (relative to the expulsion of Senator Tony Mendoza). His resignation letter was 403 words, the longest in modern history[80].

February 22, 2018

Dear Members of the State Senate and Senator pro Tempore:
I refuse to participate any further in the farcical "investigation" against me that ignores the Senate's own rules, invents processes, criteria and standards as needed, ignores due process and constitutional rights to self-defense all for the purpose of playing to election year politicking.

I shall resign my position as Senator with immediate effect as it is clear that Senate President pro Tem Kevin de León will not rest until he has my head on a platter to convince the MeToo movement of his "sincerity" in supporting the MeToo cause.

De León ordered up a secret investigation in my case, without any due process or providing me with any specific charges, access to witnesses or evidence, or any opportunity to defend myself. The results were reported using the lowest standard of proof—"more likely than not"— but asking for the highest penalty, expulsion.

---

[80] Senate Daily Journal. 22 February 2018, page 3354.

Since November 2017, the Senate Rules Committee required me to stay silent under Senate rules and also required me, disparately, to give up leadership positions, go on leave, and essentially "disappear" from Sacramento.

Now, with over a quarter of Democratic Senators either running for statewide office or under investigation, I cannot expect any fairness or justice. This is particularly true as a large number of my mostly male colleagues from either party are concerned at the prospect of being accused of "protecting" me.

Since the first opportunity arose in November 2017, I have stated my unconditional apology to any person who felt uncomfortable by my interactions with any of them. Though the summarized findings of the secret Senate investigation do not comport with my recollection or perception of the events described, I am immensely sorry if my words or actions ever made anyone feel uncomfortable. It was always my intention to be personable with my staff, show an interest in their lives outside of the office, and assist them as best I could with their career development.

I want to thank the voters in the district who elected me for their continued and strong support. I intend to canvass my district to determine my candidacy for the Senate this year. I also intend to pursue my lawsuit against the Senate for violating the constitutional rights of my district's voters and mine, dealing with me disparately compared to others charged with more serious allegations and leaving the 32nd District without representation.
Sincerely,

TONY MENDOZA
Senator, 32nd District

Assemblymember Matt Dababneh (AD-45) resigned on January 2. His resignation letter was 26 words[81].

December 29, 2017

The Honorable Anthony Rendon
Speaker of the Assembly
State Capitol, Room 219
Sacramento, California

Dear Speaker Rendon: I am revising the date of my resignation from the Assembly to be effective after close of business on January 2, 2018. Sincerely,

MATTHEW DABABNEH, Assembly Member
Forty-fifth District

2017

Assemblymember Sebastian Ridley-Thomas (AD-54) resigned on December 31. Leaving office at 30 years old, Ridley-Thomas was the youngest former legislator since 1940. His resignation letter was 182 words[82].

December 26, 2017

The Honorable Anthony Rendon
Speaker of the Assembly
State Capitol, Room 219
Sacramento, California

Speaker Rendon: After a year and a half of deteriorating health leading to five surgeries (the first in March of this year and the most recent of

---

[81] Assembly Daily Journal. 2 January 2018, page 3658.
[82] Assembly Daily Journal. 2 January 2018, page 3657.

which occurred on Monday of last week and will require an extended recovery period) and consulting my capable physician team, I have come to the conclusion that I should discontinue my reelection effort and resign my membership of the Assembly effective December 31st of this year.

I have enjoyed the near decade in the Legislature as an opportunity to advance the priorities of the residents of South and West Los Angeles. Interaction with my constituents and colleagues regularly on policy will be what I miss the most. However, recuperation and rebuilding my health are of greater import.

I thank the voters of the Fifty-fourth District for supporting me at each step of the way, my staff for ably executing high quality constituent services and innovative policy development. I also thank you for your friendship, trust and investment in me.

You can continue to count on my support of your leadership as a private citizen.
Sincerely,

SEBASTIAN RIDLEY-THOMAS, Assembly Member
Fifty-fourth District

Assemblymember Raul J. Bocanegra (AD-39) resigned on November 27. His resignation letter was 20 words[83].

November 27, 2017

The Honorable Anthony Rendon
Speaker of the Assembly
State Capitol, Room 219
Sacramento, California

---

[83] Assembly Daily Journal. 27 November 2017, page 3643.

Dear Speaker Rendon: This letter is to communicate I resign my position in the State Assembly effective immediately.
Thank you,

RAUL BOCANEGRA

Assemblymember Jimmy Gomez (AD-51) resigned on July 11 to become a member of Congress. His resignation letter was 57 words[84].

July 7, 2017

The Honorable Anthony Rendon
Speaker of the Assembly
State Capitol, Room 219
Sacramento, California

Dear Mr. Speaker: As a result of my election to the unexpired term of office for the 34th California Congressional District, I hereby respectfully submit my resignation as State Assembly Member of the 51st Assembly District. My resignation is effective upon taking the oath of office for the 34th California Congressional District on July 11, 2017. Respectfully,

JIMMY GOMEZ, Assembly Member
Fifty-first District

2016

2016 was the first year since 2004 without a single legislative resignation.

---

[84] Assembly Daily Journal. 11 July 2017, page 2509.

2015

Assemblymember Henry T. Perea resigned on December 31. His resignation letter was 135 words[85].

December 3, 2015

The Honorable Toni G. Atkins
Speaker of the Assembly
State Capitol, Room 219
Sacramento, California

Dear Madame Speaker:
It has been the honor of my life to serve the people of my hometown and Fresno County. Over the past 13 years, I have worked tirelessly with our communities to improve the quality of life in Fresno. I hereby respectfully submit my resignation as State Assemblymember of the 31st Assembly District, my resignation is effective on December 31, 2015.

I worked hard every day to deliver on the most pressing issues facing our state. This is a bittersweet moment for me, as I announce my departure from the State Legislature to pursue other career opportunities. Thank you for your leadership in the Assembly and for your commitment to the State of California. I am grateful for the opportunity to serve and look forward to continuing my advocacy for our community.
Respectfully,

HENRY T. PEREA, Assembly Member
Thirty-first District

---

[85] Assembly Daily Journal. 4 January 2016, page 3299.

State Senator Steve Knight resigned on January 5 to become a member of Congress. His resignation letter was 81 words[86].

January 5, 2015

The Honorable Kevin de León
President pro Tempore of the Senate

Dear Senator De León:
It has been an honor and privilege to be a member of this august body and to serve the constituents of the 21st Senate District. In November, I was chosen by the voters to represent them in Washington D.C., and I will be sworn-in to the 114th United States Congress on January 6, 2015.

Therefore, although bitter-sweet, I am resigning from the California State Senate effective January 5, 2015. Thank you for the comradery and friendship.
Sincerely,

STEVE KNIGHT
Senator, 21st District

State Senator Mimi Walters resigned on January 3 to become a member of Congress. Her resignation letter was 43 words[87].

January 3, 2015

The Honorable Kevin de León
President pro Tempore of the Senate

Dear Senator De León:
Effective January 3, 2015, I resign my seat as State Senator, District 37. I am grateful for the time I spent with my fellow Senators and look

---

[86] Senate Daily Journal. 5 January 2015, page 31.
[87] Senate Daily Journal. 5 January 2015, page 31.

forward to further serving the great state of California in Congress.
Respectfully,

MIMI WALTERS
Senator, 37th District

State Senator Mark DeSaulnier resigned on January 2 to become a member of Congress. His resignation letter was 92 words[88].

December 23, 2014

The Honorable Kevin de León
President pro Tempore of the Senate

Dear Senator De León:
It has been an honor to represent the Seventh Senate District for the last six years. As you know, I was elected to the 11th Congressional District in November. So it is with great sadness and joy that I write to tender my resignation from the State Senate effective at 11:59 p.m. on Friday, January 2, 2015. I will miss all of my colleagues, the staff at the Senate Desk and the Senate Sergeants and all the people that make the Senate a wonderful place to work.
Sincerely,

MARK DESAULNIER
Senator, 7th District

---

[88] <u>Senate Daily Journal</u>. 5 January 2015, page 31.

2014

State Senator Rod Wright resigned on September 22. Wright resigned after being convicted of eight felony charges relating to providing a false address when he ran for the legislature. Governor Brown pardoned Wright in 2018. His resignation letter was 16 words, the shortest in modern history[89].

September 15, 2014

Dear Mr. Schmidt:
Effective September 22, 2014, I hereby resign from the California State Senate.
Sincerely,

RODERICK D. WRIGHT

Assemblymember Mike Morrell resigned on April 3 to become a State Senator. His resignation letter was 54 words[90].

April 1, 2014

Dear Mr. Speaker:
As a result of my election to the unexpired term of office for the 23rd Senatorial District, I hereby respectfully submit my resignation as State Assemblymember of the 40th Assembly District. My resignation is effective upon taking the oath of office for the 23rd Senate District on April 3, 2014.
Respectfully,

MIKE MORRELL
Assembly Member Fortieth District

---

[89] Senate Daily Journal. 17 September 2014, page 5029.
[90] Assembly Daily Journal. 3 April 2014, page 4324.

2013

State Senator Bill Emmerson resigned on December 1 to become a State Senator. His resignation letter was 46 words[91].

November 8, 2013

The Honorable Darrell Steinberg
President pro Tempore, California State Senate

Dear Mr. President pro Tempore,
I hereby resign my seat in the State Senate, effective December 1, 2013.

It has been an honor to serve in this great institution alongside colleagues who I will always count as friends.
Thank you for your time and consideration.
Respectfully,

Bill Emmerson
State Senator, 23rd District

Assemblymember Holly Mitchell resigned on September 26 to become a State Senator. Her resignation letter was 173 words[92].

September 25, 2013

Dearest Speaker Pérez:
It is indeed with mixed emotions that I submit this letter as my official resignation from the California State Assembly, representing the good people of the 54th Assembly District. My resignation shall take effect immediately upon my taking the oath of office to serve in the State Senate, representing the 26th District, on September 26, 2013. It has been suggested by historians and such that I use this official document to chronicle my work in the Assembly. I have chosen, however, to let

---

[91] Senate Daily Journal. 27 November 2013, page 2496.
[92] Assembly Daily Journal. 26 September 2013, page 3385.

my work—our work, as conscientious policy makers who remain deeply committed to the well-being of ALL Californians—speak for itself:

• An on-time balanced budget that invests strategically in core services for vulnerable communities.
• Meaningful support for low-income working families and their children.
• Expansion of critical health services for those who've gone without for far too long.
• Protection of the fundamental rights of women, immigrants, workers, children, and those serving in the juvenile and adult prison system.

With that, I will simply say, PEACE OUT!
Respectfully Submitted,

HOLLY J. MITCHELL
Assembly Member Fifty-fourth District

Assemblymember Bob Blumenfield resigned on June 30 to become a member of the Los Angeles City Council. His resignation letter was 49 words[93].

June 30, 2013

Dear Mr. Speaker: As a result of my election to the Los Angeles Council District 3, I hereby respectfully submit my resignation as State Assemblymember of the 45th Assembly District. My resignation is effective upon taking the oath of office for the City Council on June 30, 2013.
Sincerely,

BOB BLUMENFIELD
Assembly Member Forty-fifth District

---

[93] Assembly Daily Journal. 1 July 2013, page 2232.

State Senator Curren D. Price resigned on June 30 to become a member of the Los Angeles City Council. His resignation letter was 246 words[94].

June 30, 2013

Dear President Pro Tem Steinberg
I hereby resign effective June 30, 2013 from the California State Senate to be sworn in as Los Angeles City Councilman for City Council District 9. Representing the 26th Senate District these past five years in the California State Senate has been the most gratifying experience of my decades-long career in public service.

Under your leadership, we were able to pass the kind of laws that not only protect the interests of all Californians but also improve the quality of life for generations to come.

As you know I have a keen interest in small business development and while serving in the Legislature I authored legislation that increased opportunities for small businesses to compete for state contracts and offered incentives for creating new jobs.

This type of legislation sparks economic growth, encourages innovation, opens the doors for diversity in public contracting and stimulates our state's economy. I also successfully carried bills that expanded health care, increased educational opportunities, promoted civic engagement and supported the Arts. I am proud of these accomplishments.

While I am sad about leaving the Senate, I am excited about going home. I was born in the 9th District of Los Angeles and I have seen that community suffer a serious decline.

---

[94] Senate Daily Journal. 1 July 2013, pages 1615-1616.

I know the skills I have learned in my years working with you and under your able leadership will help me build the consensus and momentum that is necessary to create a "New 9th District".
Sincerely,

Curren Price Jr.

Assemblymember Norma J. Torres resigned on May 20 to become a State Senator. Her resignation letter was 53 words[95].

May 16, 2013

Dear Mr. Speaker: As a result of my election to the unexpired term of office for the 32nd Senatorial District, I hereby respectfully submit my resignation as State Assemblymember of the 52nd Assembly District. My resignation is effective upon taking oath of office for the 32nd Senate District on May 20, 2013.
Respectfully,

NORMA J. TORRES, Assembly Member
Fifty-second District

State Senator Michael Rubio resigned on February 22. His resignation letter was 82 words[96].

February 22, 2013

Dear Senate President pro Tem Steinberg:
In order to spend more quality time with my growing family, I have decided to step away from my official capacity as Senator. As such, please accept this letter as my resignation from the California State Senate, effective immediately.

It has been a distinct honor and privilege to serve in the Legislature.

---

[95] Assembly Daily Journal. 20 May 2013, page 1493.
[96] Senate Daily Journal. 25 February 2013, page 217.

I am grateful for the support you and your staff have always provided me on behalf of the citizens of our great state.
Sincerely,

Michael J. Rubio
State Senator, Sixteenth District

State Senator Juan Vargas resigned on January 2 after being elected to Congress. His resignation letter was 124 words[97].

January 1, 2013

Dear President pro Tempore Steinberg:
I hereby respectfully tender my resignation as California State Senator for the 40th Senate District, effective January 2, 2013 at 5:00pm.

As you know, I was elected on November 6, 2012 to serve as the United States Representative for the California 51st Congressional District. I will be sworn into office as the U.S. Representative for 51st Congressional District on January 3, 2013.

It has been an honor and a privilege to serve alongside you and my fellow colleagues in the California State Senate and to represent the constituents of the 40th Senate District. I look forward to continuing to work with you and my successor to further strengthen the relationship between the State of California and federal government.
Sincerely,

JUAN VARGAS
State Senator
40th Senate District

---

[97] <u>Senate Daily Journal</u>. 7 January 2013, page 39.

State Senator Gloria Negrete-McLeod resigned on January 2 to become a Member of Congress. Her resignation letter was 50 words[98].

December 27, 2012

Dear President pro Tempore Steinberg:
It has been an honor serving the constituents of California's 32nd Senate District, so it is with great sadness and joy that I ask you to accept my resignation as an elected member of the California State Senate, effective January 2nd, 2013, at 11:59PM.
Respectfully,

Gloria Negrete McLeod
32nd Senate District

2012

State Senator Doug La Malfa resigned on September 1 prior to being elected to Congress. His resignation came at the end of session, four months before his term in Congress began, which allowed his successor to be seated near the beginning of the following session (in January) rather than as late as May. His resignation letter was 230 words[99].

August 31, 2012

Dear Senator Steinberg,
It has been my sincere honor to serve as the State Senator for the Fourth District and the 12 wonderful North State Counties. I am proud of the work I have done on behalf of my constituents both legislatively and in helping them navigate the numerous hurdles in State Government.

---

[98] Senate Daily Journal. 7 January 2013, page 39.
[99] Senate Daily Journal. 1 September 2012, pages 5132-5133.

When I announced my intention to seek election to the first congressional district earlier this year, I knew there would be a possibility of a special election to fill the vacancy that would be created if I were successful. While that election is still undecided, I care too deeply about the constituents I serve, the counties I represent and the taxpayers I've fought for to saddle them with a series of costly special elections.

I have consulted expert outside counsel and have been informed that were my resignation submitted today, the election to fill the vacancy in Senate District Four could be consolidated with the November 6, 2012 General Election, thereby saving the people of my district significant and scarce tax dollars.

Additionally, by holding the election on November 6th, a new Senator will be seated before early January so that the North State will have a strong voice during a very active portion of the new legislative year.

Therefore, I resign as State Senator of California's Fourth Senate District, effective upon final adjournment of session.
Respectfully,

DOUG LA MALFA

2011

Assemblymember Ted Gaines resigned on January 6 to become a State Senator. His resignation letter was 37 words[100].

January 6, 2011

Dear Mr. Speaker: I hereby respectfully submit my resignation as State Assemblyman for the 4th Assembly District. My resignation is effective

---

[100] Assembly Daily Journal. 6 January 2011, page 128.

upon taking the oath of office for the 1st Senate District on January 6, 2011.
Sincerely,

TED GAINES, Assembly Member
Fourth District

2010

State Senator George Runner resigned on December 21 after being elected to the State Board of Equalization. His inauguration ended Sean Wallentine's three days as an acting member of the Board (which was the shortest service of any California constitutional officer)[101]. His resignation letter was 83 words[102].

> *December 17, 2010*
>
> *Dear President pro Tempore Steinberg,*
> *As you are aware, I was recently elected to the Board of Equalization to represent the 2nd District and therefore must resign my senate seat effective the close of business on December 21, 2010.*
>
> *I have greatly enjoyed my tenure as a state legislator as it has been a pleasure serving the constituents of the 17th Senate District. I look forward to continuing that service on the Board of Equalization for all constituents of the 2nd District.*
> *Sincerely,*
>
> *GEORGE C. RUNNER, JR.*
> *Senator, 17th District*

---

[101] The three days that Sean Wallentine served as an acting member of the Board of Equalization in 2011 broke the record previously set by the five days Milton S. Latham served as Governor in 1860.
[102] Senate Daily Journal. 3 January 2011, page 44.

Assemblymember Sam Blakeslee resigned on August 23 after being elected to the State Senate. His resignation letter was 54 words[103].

August 20, 2010

Dear Speaker Pérez:
As a result of my election to the unexpired term of office for the 15th Senatorial District, I hereby respectfully submit my resignation as State Assemblymember of the 33rd Assembly District. My resignation is effective upon taking the oath of office for the 15th Senate District on August 23, 2010.
Sincerely,

SAM BLAKESLEE, Assembly Member
Thirty-third District

Assemblymember Bill Emmerson resigned on June 9 to become a State Senator. His resignation letter was 54 words[104].

June 9, 2010

Dear Mr. Speaker: As a result of my election to the unexpired term of office for the 37th Senatorial District, I hereby respectfully submit my resignation as State Assemblymember of the 63rd Assembly District. My resignation is effective upon taking the oath of office for the 37th Senate District on June 9, 2010.
Respectfully,

BILL EMMERSON, Assembly Member
Sixty-third District

---

[103] Assembly Daily Journal. 23 August 2010, page 6461.
[104] Assembly Daily Journal. 10 June 2010, page 5620.

State Senator Abel Maldonado resigned on April 27 after the State Senate after being appointed Lt. Governor. His resignation letter was 82 words[105].

> *April 27, 2010*
>
> *Dear Senator Steinberg:*
> *Due to my confirmation to fill the vacancy in Lieutenant Governor's office, I hereby resign my seat as the State Senator for the 15th Senate District effective today.*
>
> *I have thoroughly enjoyed my service as a legislator both in the Assembly and Senate. Serving my constituents has always been my number one priority. I now look forward to the new challenges that come with the office of the Lieutenant Governor and serving the citizens of the entire state.*
> *Sincerely,*
>
> *ABEL MALDONADO*
> *Senator, 15th District*

Assemblymember Paul Krekorian resigned on January 5 to become a member of the Los Angeles City Council. His resignation letter was 214 words[106].

> *January 4, 2010*
>
> *Dear Mme. Speaker: As a result of my election to the unexpired term of office for the Second District seat on the Los Angeles City Council, I hereby respectfully submit my resignation as State Assemblymember for the 43rd Assembly District. My resignation is effective upon my taking the oath of office for the City Council on January 5, 2010.*

---

[105] Senate Daily Journal. 27 April 2010, page 3357.
[106] Assembly Daily Journal. 4 January 2010, page 3648.

*It has been an incredible privilege to serve as a member of this house
and to help shape the future of our state by creating jobs, improving
our environment and strengthening public safety. I am very proud to
have had important legislative successes even under historically
difficult fiscal conditions, including instituting the state's first-ever film
and television incentive, reducing pollution in our oceans and making
neighborhoods safer by allowing landlords to evict dangerous
criminals. It has been an honor to work under your historic Speakership
and with a Caucus that achieved success under circumstances that
were often turbulent and challenging.*

*I will look back on my time in the Assembly warmly as I consider the
important task ahead as a member of the Los Angeles City Council. I
am eager to begin addressing the urgent challenges the city is facing,
and I look forward to working with you closely in doing so.*
Very truly yours,

PAUL KREKORIAN, Assembly Member
Forty-third District

2009

State Senator John J. Benoit resigned on November 30 to accept
appointment as a Riverside County Supervisor. His resignation letter
was 182 words[107].

November 8, 2009

Dear Mr. Steinberg:
As you are aware, I was appointed by Governor Schwarzenegger to the
Riverside County Board of Supervisors to represent the Fourth District.
I am very honored by the governor's appointment, however, I have
been advised that a short deferral of my resignation may result in a

---

[107] Senate Daily Journal. 30 November 2009, page 2562.

significant savings to taxpayers. A slightly later date would potentially allow the consolidation of the Senate special election with the statewide June primary.

Therefore, I hereby request that you disregard my previous letter of resignation. With your concurrence, I will resign my seat as a California State Senator for the 37th Senate District effective Monday, November 30, 2009. I will be sworn in on Tuesday, December 1, 2009.

Once again, allow me to say that I have thoroughly enjoyed my service as a state legislator. I am particularly pleased that I was able to support your outstanding efforts to address California's water crisis before leaving the senate. My legislative experience has prepared me well to address future challenges on a local level as a member of the Riverside County Board of Supervisors.
Sincerely,

JOHN J. BENOIT

Assemblymember Mike Duvall resigned on September 9th. His resignation letter, at 22 words, is the only known retroactive resignation in state history[108].

September 10, 2009

Dear Madame Speaker:
I hereby respectfully submit my resignation as State Assemblymember of the 72nd Assembly District, effective September 9, 2009.
Respectfully,

MIKE DUVALL, Assembly Member
Seventy-second District

---

[108] Assembly Daily Journal. 10 September 2009, page 3254.

Assemblymember Curren D. Price resigned on June 8 following his election to the State Senate. His resignation letter was 54 words[109].

> June 8, 2009
>
> Dear Mme. Speaker:
> As a result of my election to the unexpired term of office for the 26th Senatorial District, I hereby respectfully submit my resignation as State Assemblymember of the 51st Assembly District.
>
> My resignation is effective upon taking the oath of office for the 26th Senate District on June 8, 2009.
> Respectfully,
>
> CURREN D. PRICE, JR., Assembly Member
> Fifty-first District

2008

State Senator Mark Ridley-Thomas resigned on November 30 to become a Los Angeles County Supervisor. His resignation letter was 302 words[110].

> *November 25, 2008*
>
> *Dear Lieutenant Governor Garamendi:*
> *Please accept my resignation as an elected member of the California State Senate representing the people of the 26th District. My resignation is effective at 12:00 a.m. (midnight) Sunday, November 30, 2008. I formally resign to assume my position as a newly-elected member of the Los Angeles County Board of Supervisors representing*

---

[109] Assembly Daily Journal. 8 June 2009, page 2098.
[110] Senate Daily Journal. 25 November 2008, pages 5699-5700.

the people of the Second District at 12:00 p.m. (noon) on Monday, December 1, 2008.

So as to minimize the local government expense associated with filling the 26th District Senate seat I am vacating, and pursuant to state law, it is my sincere hope that Governor Schwarzenegger will issue a proclamation calling for a special election for voters to choose a new 26th Senate District representative be scheduled to coincide with the municipal elections in the City and County of Los Angeles on March 3, with a runoff election to be held on May 19, 2009, if no candidate receives a majority of the votes cast during the March primary election.

It is my hope that these elections can be consolidated on the same ballot already on our local government elections calendar, thereby saving taxpayers an estimated $1.5 million in election administration expenses, and at the same time, mitigating voter fatigue.

It has been an honor to serve the constituents of the 26th Senate District. I have enjoyed working with my Senate colleagues and legislative staff whose commitment to public service remains an inspiration for my own work. Although I am moving to a new public service assignment, I look forward to engaging members of the Legislature on important policy issues on an ongoing basis, especially members in the Senate—the body for which I have the utmost respect and regard—in our continuing effort to make government work for the people we represent.
With hope,

MARK RIDLEY-THOMAS
26th Senate District

2007

Assemblymember Laura Richardson resigned on September 4 after her election to Congress. At the time, the 261 days she served was the shortest tenure by a female legislator. Her resignation letter was 54 words[111].

> *September 4, 2007*
>
> *Dear Mr. Speaker: As a result of my election to the unexpired term of office for the 37th Congressional District, I hereby respectfully submit my resignation as State Assembly Member of the 55th Assembly District.*
>
> *My resignation effective upon taking the oath of office for the 37 Congressional District on September 4, 2007.*
> *Respectfully,*
>
> *LAURA RICHARDSON, Assembly Member*
> *Fifty-fifth District*

Assemblymember Richard Alarcon resigned on March 16. His resignation after 107 days in the Assembly was the fastest voluntary departure by an Assemblymember since Harry S. Wanzer left in 1903. His resignation letter was 109 words[112].

> *March 16, 2007*
>
> *Dear Mr. Speaker:*
> *I hereby resign my Assembly District 39 seat, effective today.*
>
> *As you are aware, the Los Angeles City General Election is scheduled for May 15, 2007, and by my resigning today, the Assembly District 39*

---

[111] Assembly Daily Journal. 4 September 2007, page 2832.
[112] Assembly Daily Journal. 19 March 2007, page 627.

election can be consolidated with the city election, saving taxpayers over $100,000.00. The consolidated election will also serve to draw more voters to the polls. The consolidated election will additionally assure the residents of Assembly District 39 that a replacement Assembly Member will be elected and seated during the crucial state budget deliberations.

I thank you for your continued assistance to me and the residents of Assembly District 39.
Yours truly,

RICHARD ALARCÓN, Assembly Member
Thirty-ninth District

2006

Assemblymember Tom Harman resigned on June 12 to take a seat in the State Senate. His resignation letter was 54 words[113].

June 7, 2006

Dear Mr. Speaker:
As a result of my election to the unexpired term of office for the 35th Senatorial District, I hereby respectfully submit my resignation as State Assemblymember of the 67th Assembly District. My resignation is effective upon taking the oath of office for the 35th Senate District on June 12, 2006.
Respectfully,

TOM HARMAN, Assembly Member
Sixty-seventh District

---

[113] Assembly Daily Journal. 12 June 2006, page 6034.

Total Prior Legislative Service

Session	Total Prior Service	Session	Total Prior Service
2021-22	651 years	1961	886 years
2019-20	557 years	1959	798 years
2017-18	431 years	1957	846 years
2015-16	398 years	1955	826 years
2013-14	424 years	1953	864 years
2011-12	475 years	1951	803 years
2009-10	481 years	1949	795 years
2007-08	500 years	1947	836 years
2005-06	656 years	1945	822 years
2003-04	531 years	1943	642 years
2001-02	593 years	1941	609 years
1999-00	612 years	1939	566 years
1997-98	739 years	1937	496 years
1995-96	978 years	1935	416 years
1993-94	1110 years	1933	478 years
1991-92	1265 years	1931	572 years
1989-90	1189 years	1929	612 years
1987-88	1014 years	1927	506 years
1985-86	1170 years	1925	436 years
1983-84	747 years	1923	402 years
1981-82	760 years	1921	354 years
1979-80	770 years	1919	274 years
1977-78	820 years	1917	238 years
1975-76	870 years	1915	247 years
1973-74	927 years	1913	267 years
1971-72	900 years	1911	255 years
1969-70	815 years	1909	234 years
1967-68	711 years	1907	243 years
1965	836 years	1905	224 years
1963	698 years	1903	195 years

Prior Legislative Service

> "Some legislative experience is necessary to learn the details of the lawmaking procedure, to develop political tactics, and to acquire the skill in debate and committee activities so necessary to successful accomplishment."
> - Assemblyman Dewey Anderson[114]

One interesting way to compare different sessions of the legislature is to look at the combined length of prior legislative service.[115] Rather than looking at a specific lawmaker, you can see the entire institution from a single perspective.

The legislatures of the 1950s to 1970s, which established a number of major public works projects and expanded California's university systems, tended to hover generally in the 800-year range. The term-limits era saw the count drop from the all-time high of more than 12 centuries down to under 400 years in 2015-16, the lowest point in the past century. Since then, we've been seeing the prior service numbers rise as members began staying longer (and former lawmakers returned to the legislature).

Probably the most exceptional session of the prior century was that of 1911. Those 120 members arrived with 257 years of prior legislative experience and, in just 114 days of session, established women's suffrage in California and created the recall, referendum, and initiative[116].

---

[114] California State Government (Stanford University Press; 1942), page 84.

[115] Just to be clear on what we're counting here: an incoming freshman legislator brings zero years of prior experience, while a second-term Assemblymember has 2 years from their first term.

[116] For more information, see Story of the Session of the California Legislature of 1911 by Franklin Hichborn (James H. Barry Company; 1911).

Historic Deans of the Senate

Year	Senator(s)
2013-	Jim Nielsen
2011-2012	Elaine Alquist, Bob Dutton, Christine Kehoe, Alan Lowenthal, and Joe Simitian
2009-2010	Gloria Romero
2005-2008	Don Perata
2003-2004	Ross Johnson
2001-2002	Maurice Johannessen
1999-2000	Patrick Johnston
1997-1998	Ralph C. Dills
1989-1996	Ralph C. Dills, Nicholas Petris, and Al Alquist
1987-1988	Ralph Dills, Nicholas Petris, Al Alquist, and H.L. Richardson
1981-1986	Walter W. Stiern
1977-1980	Albert S. Rodda
1963-1976	Randolph Collier
1961-1962	Randolph Collier and Charlie Brown
1957-1960	James J. McBride
1953-1956	Harry L. Parkman
1951-1952	Harry L. Parkman and Harold J. Powers
1947-1950	Ralph E. Swing
1935-1946	Herbert W. Slater
1929-1934	Herbert C. Jones and Arthur H. Breed
1917-1928	Benjamin F. Rush

Dean of the Senate

"It is the role of the Dean to teach what Senatorial Courtesy is and in fact practice it as an example each day."
- Senator Jim Nielsen[117]

The Dean is an honorary title given to the member of each house who has served the longest. Because the members of the first Legislature all had the same level of prior experience, it wasn't until 1852 that the Senate had its first Dean, Senator David Broderick, who had three years of service.

Other Deans of the Senate have included Randolph Collier, who was the Dean for 14 years and was long remembered as the "Father of California's Highway System". Ralph Dills, one of the longest-serving members from 1987 to 1998, was a brother of Clayton Dills, who was Dean of the Assembly in 1963 to 1966.

Benjamin Franklin Rush, Dean of the Senate for 12 years, was elected to the Senate after promising his constituents that he, "wouldn't make no speeches." Accordingly, he made only one floor speech during his years in the Senate. That speech was;

> *"Mr. President, now about this bill: A man come over to Napa give me this bill. He said it was a good bill. I've knowed the man 30 years and he never lied to me yet. The committee says it's a good bill and I hope you'll all vote for it."*[118]

Greg Schmidt, longtime Secretary of the Senate, kept copies of the book The California Legislature on hand in his office just off the Senate Floor in order to pass along the wisdom of short speeches to newer Senators.

---

[117] Email to the author (December 30, 2016)
[118] The California Legislature by Joseph Allan Beek (California State Printing Office; 1950), page 145.

Historic Deans of the Assembly

Year	Assemblymember(s)
2021-	24 Members of the Class of 2012[119]
2019-2020	28 Members of the Class of 2012
2017-2018	31 Members of the Class of 2012 and Anna Caballero
2015-2016	Mike Gatto
2013-2014	14 Members of the Class of 2008
2009-2012	Charles Calderon
2007-2008	Mervyn Dymally
2005-2006	Johan Klehs
2003-2004	Tim Leslie
1997-2002	Louis J. Papan
1995-1996	John Vasconcellos
1983-1995	Willie L. Brown Jr.
1981-1982	Leroy F. Greene
1979-1980	John T. Knox
1967-1978	Vincent Thomas
1963-1966	Clayton A. Dills
1957-1962	Augustus F. Hawkins
1952-1956	Thomas Maloney
1949-1951	Ernest C. Crowley
1943-1949	Samuel L. Heisinger
1939-1942	Eleanor Miller
1935-1938	William B. Hornblower
1932-1934	Frederick M. Roberts
1931-1932	Fred Hawes, Harry Morrison and T. M. Wright
1921-1930	Frank L. Coombs

---

[119] Currently, the longest-serving Assemblymembers are: Bigelow, Bloom, Bonta, Chau, Cooley, Daly, Frazier, Garcia, Gray, Holden, Jones-Sawyer Jr., Levine, Maienschein, Medina, Mullin, Nazarian, Patterson, Quirk, Rendon, Salas, Stone, Ting, Waldron, and Weber.

Dean of the Assembly

> **"Willie Brown taught me how a committee should be run, how to treat witnesses fairly but move things along and how to engage every Member in the process."**
> - *Senator Bill Leonard*[120]

In the Assembly, the higher turnover of membership has meant that the honor of being the longest serving member of the house has rotated more frequently than in the Senate.

The first Dean of the Assembly was Jose M. Covarrubias, who became the longest-serving member of the lower house by serving a third one-year term. He held onto the title, also being the first to serve a fourth, fifth, sixth, seventh, eighth, and ninth term.

Covarrubias lived a fascinating life which included owning Santa Catalina Island for several years, being elected to the state's first constitutional convention by two different districts, and having the unique distinction of being the only person to resign from the State Assembly twice.

Other fascinating Assembly Deans included Frederick M. Roberts and Ernest Crowley. Roberts made history in 1919 as the first African-American to serve in the California Legislature. Crowley, who arrived a decade later, was the state's first blind lawmaker[121]. From 1929 to 1943, Crowley's wife Georgia attended session with him, sitting at his desk on the Assembly Floor[122]. In 1941, the Assembly voted to make Georgia an honorary Assemblymember[123], one of only two people known to receive that honor.

---

[120] Email to the author (January 9, 2021)
[121] According to his biography in the <u>California Blue Book</u>, "at the age of eleven years, Mr. Crowley accidentally suffered the loss of his eyesight while duck hunting."
[122] Assembly Daily Journal, 7 June 1941, page 4126.
[123] House Resolution 257 (1941)

Legislators with the Longest Total Service[124]

#	Legislator	Years	#	Legislator	Years
1	Ralph C. Dills	42.35	29	John L. Burton	26.19
2	Milton Marks	37.92	30	Lester A. McMillan	26.00
3	Randolph Collier	37.92	31	Ross Johnson	26.00
4	Nicholas C. Petris	37.92	32	Charles J. Conrad	26.00
5	Vincent Thomas	37.92	33	Bill Greene	25.92
6	John Vasconcellos	37.92	34	William A. Craven	25.44
7	Herbert W. Slater	36.62	35	Teresa P. Hughes	25.38
8	Leroy F. Greene	35.92	36	Bill Lockyer	25.25
9	Hugh M. Burns	34.00	37	Ruben S. Ayala	24.87
10	Charles W. Lyon	34.00	38	Samuel L. Heisinger	24.73
11	Alfred E. Alquist	33.92	39	Chris N. Jespersen	24.13
12	Hugh P. Donnelly	32	**40**	**Jim Nielsen**	**24.01**
13	Thomas A. Maloney	32	41	Herschel Rosenthal	24
14	John L. E. Collier	31.92	42	Charles Brown	24
15	Newton R. Russell	31.92	43	Benjamin F. Rush	24
16	Willie L. Brown	30.96	44	Vernon Kilpatrick	24
17	Harry L. Parkman	30	45	David G. Kelley	24
18	Bradford S. Crittenden	30	46	Nelson S. Dilworth	24
19	Donald L. Grunsky	29.92	47	Tom Bane	24
20	Robert G. Beverly	29.58	48	Bill Leonard	24
21	James J. McBride	28.46	49	Richard J. Dolwig	24
22	Ralph E. Swing	28	50	Clayton A. Dills	24
23	Augustus F. Hawkins	28	51	Byron Sher	24
24	Frank Lanterman	27.92	52	Arthur H. Breed Jr.	24
25	Walter W. Stiern	27.92	53	Jim Costa	24
26	David A. Roberti	27.92	54	Daniel Boatwright	23.92
27	Kenneth L. Maddy	27.38	55	Pauline L. Davis	23.92
28	Wadie P. Deddeh	26.63	56	John F. Foran	23.92

---

[124] **Bold** indicates currently serving. *Italicized* indicates deceased.

Legislative Tenure

The turnover of legislators has frequently been extremely high. Since statehood, more than half of California's legislators left after serving two years or less. Occasionally, outliers would settle into the Legislature and stay for decades.

Ralph C. Dills, the longest-serving legislator in state history, was first elected in 1938 and served more than a decade in the Assembly before resigning to become a Los Angeles County municipal judge. After 17 years on the bench, he was elected to the Senate in 1966 and served there for nearly 32 years, leaving office in 1998.

Jesse S. Pitzer was the shortest-serving legislator ever. His opponent in the 1852 election, W. C. Martin (a Whig), was elected to the State Assembly and sworn into office on January 3rd. On January 19th, Pitzer (a Democrat) successfully challenged Martin's election with evidence that he had received more votes.

Martin was removed from office and Pitzer was sworn in. On the third day he was in office, a revised final vote count arrived that declared Martin the winner. After three days in office, Pitzer became a former legislator on January 21st.

List of Longest Serving Assemblymembers[125]

Most people today are familiar with only a few of these names like Willie Brown or John Burton, but almost all of these people were giants of California law who made the state you recognize today.

#	Assemblymember	Years	#	Assemblymember	Years
1	Vincent Thomas	37.92	26	Charles W. Meyers	20.00
2	John L. E. Collier	31.92	27	Charles W. Lyon	20.00
3	**Willie L. Brown**	**30.96**	28	Eleanor Miller	20.00
4	John Vasconcellos	29.92	**29**	**Tom Bates**	**20.00**
5	Augustus F. Hawkins	28.00	30	Louis J. Papan	19.92
6	Frank D. Lanterman	27.92	31	Carlos Bee	19.92
7	Charles J. Conrad	26.00	32	Leroy F. Greene	19.92
8	Lester A. McMillan	26.00	33	Ralph M. Brown	18.71
9	Samuel L. Heisinger	24.73	34	Don A. Allen Sr.	18.46
10	Tom Bane	24.00	35	Thomas J. Doyle	18.35
11	Clayton A. Dills	24.00	**36**	**John L. Burton**	**18.19**
12	Thomas A. Maloney	24.00	37	Stan Statham	18.00
13	Vernon Kilpatrick	24.00	38	Montivel A. Burke	18.00
14	Pauline L. Davis	23.92	39	Frank L. Coombs	18.00
15	Ernest C. Crowley	23.73	40	William B. Hornblower	18.00
16	Lloyd W. Lowrey	22.00	41	Roy J. Nielsen	18.00
17	George A. Clarke	22.00	42	Thomas M. Hannigan	18.00
18	Edward M. Gaffney	22.00	43	Wm. Byron Rumford	18.00
19	Carley V. Porter	21.95	**44**	**Gordon W. Duffy**	**17.92**
20	Peter R. Chacon	21.92	45	Teresa P. Hughes	17.38
21	Frank P. Belotti	21.92	46	Edwin Z'berg	16.65
22	Edward E. Elliott	21.75	47	Ross Johnson	16.42
23	William H. Lancaster	20.48	48	Robert W. Crown	16.37
24	Richard H. McCollister	20.00	49	Richard Mountjoy	16.15
25	John T. Knox	20.00	50	Charles E. Chapel	16.13

---

[125] Names in **BOLD** indicate living former legislators.

List of Longest Serving State Senators[126]

Reaching 20 years in the State Senate in January 2021, Jim Nielsen is currently the 26th-longest-serving Senator in state history. By the end of the session (his last), he will have moved up to 22nd.

#	State Senator	Years	#	State Senator	Years
1	Randolph Collier	37.92	**26**	**Jim Nielsen[127]**	**20.01**
2	Herbert W. Slater	32.62	27	Bradford S. Crittenden	20
3	Ralph C. Dills	31.92	28	Robert G. Beverly	20
4	Nicholas C. Petris	29.92	29	William A. Craven	20
5	Alfred E. Alquist	29.92	30	Arthur H. Breed Jr.	20
6	Milton Marks	29.31	31	Will R. Sharkey	20
7	Hugh M. Burns	28.00	32	Robert B. Presley	20
8	Ralph E. Swing	28.00	33	Thomas R. McCormack	20
9	Walter W. Stiern	27.92	34	William P. Rich	20
10	Ruben S. Ayala	24.87	35	John F. McCarthy	20
11	James J. McBride	24.46	36	Diane E. Watson	20
12	Hugh P. Donnelly	24.00	37	Alan Short	19.92
13	Harry L. Parkman	24.00	38	John W. Holmdahl	19.79
14	Benjamin F. Rush	24.00	39	Stephen P. Teale	19.56
15	Charles Brown	24.00	40	Kenneth L. Maddy	19.46
16	Donald L. Grunsky	23.92	41	Alan Robbins	18.73
17	David A. Roberti	23.35	42	Edward I. Wolfe	18.23
18	Newton R. Russell	22.88	43	Chris N. Jespersen	18.13
19	Albert S. Rodda	22.08	44	Luther E. Gibson	18
20	Arthur H. Breed	22.00	45	Bill Greene	17.67
21	Herbert C. Jones	22.00	46	J. M. Inman	17.67
22	H. L. Richardson	21.92	47	John G. Schmitz	17.42
23	Benjamin F. Langford	21.00	48	Charles H. Deuel	16.56
24	Harold J. Powers	20.77	49	Edwin J. Regan	16.02
25	George Miller Jr.	20.02	50	14 Senators	16.00

[126] **BOLD** indicates currently serving. *Italicized* indicates deceased.
[127] Jim Nielsen's tenure is as of January 15, 2021.

Shortest Serving Assemblymembers

Of the thousands of people who have served in the Assembly, only a handful have served for less than a full year. One of the most interesting is Assemblyman Barnabas Collins of Butte County, who died in office just four days into his first term.

When the 1901 legislative session began, Collins was appointed as a member of the Counties and County Boundaries Committee, the Roads and Highways Committee, and as Chairman of the Committee on Fish and Game.

A week after being sworn into office, he died suddenly of pneumonia.

In a eulogy delivered on the Assembly Floor, Grove Johnson noted;

> *"For twenty-one years I had known Mr. Collins, and in every relation the man proved his worth as a father, as a husband, as a friend, as a citizen. Here in this Assembly we have not had time to understand his worth. We have not been able to appreciate the dignity of his character and his indomitable perseverance."* [128]

Six decades later, his name was repurposed by writers of the ABC television show "Dark Shadows" (1966-1971) for a vampire. In 2018, Warner Bros. released a horror-comedy movie based on the show starring Johnny Depp as Collins, a vampire freed after being locked in a coffin for two hundred years, who moves in with his descendants who now live in his old mansion.

As of late 2020, Assemblyman Collins' grave at the Sacramento City Cemetery is undisturbed and he remains in the ground. He is not a vampire.

---

[128] Assembly Daily Journal, 16 January 1901, page 92.

List of Shortest Serving Assemblymembers[129]

	Assemblymember	Year	Days	Reason for leaving office
1	Jesse S. Pitzer	1853	3	Lost election re-recount[130]
2	William B. Dickenson	1849	4	Lost election recount
3	Barnabas Collins	1901	4	Died
4	William Van Voorhies	1849	6	Resigned
5	Dana P. Eicke	1935	20	Died
6	C. J. Freeman	1851	32	Resigned
7	**Adrian C. Fondse**	1981	35	Lost election recount
8	A. D. Duffey	1903	37	Lost election recount
9	P. B. Cornwall	1850	43	Resigned
10	Alfred Wheeler	1850	47	Term ended
11	William Grove Deal	1850	50	Term ended
12	J. B. McDonald	1895	53	Lost election recount
13	Richard W. Heath	1849	65	Resigned
14	J. W. Van Benschoten	1850	66	Resigned
15	Horace W. Carpentier	1853	67	Seat declared vacant
16	Charles A. Hughes	1883	68	Died
17	Harry S. Wanzer	1903	71	Resigned
18	J. F. Stephens	1849	79	Resigned
19	C. V. R. Lee	1853	81	Resigned
20	**Richard Alarcon**	2007	102	Resigned
21	John C. Bell	1860	104	Died (Murdered)
22	Oliver S. Witherby	1849	117	Resigned
23	**Jeff Marston**	1990	177	Term ended
24	Domer F. Power	1956	180	Term ended
25	Mike Gordon	2005	202	Died
26	**Laura Richardson**	2007	261	Resigned
27	A. W. Way	1949	320	Resigned
28	Don Anderson	1958	331	Term ended
29	Jimmie Hicks	1961	362	Died

---

[129] Names in **BOLD** indicate living former legislators.
[130] Pitzer had lost the initial vote count, won a recount, and then lost the re-recount.

List of Shortest Serving State Senators[131]

In proportion to its relative size, the Senate has had slightly fewer short-serving members, with 20 having served less than a year. The short terms resulted from a number of causes; Nathaniel Bennett and former U.S. Senator Alexander Outlaw Anderson resigned from the State Senate to become California Supreme Court Justices. Senators Porter, Burns, and Tauzer died in office and Senator Eli Wright was expelled after eight weeks for accepting bribes.

	Senator	Year	Days	Reason for leaving office
1	Nathaniel Bennett	1849	5	Resigned
2	Jonas Spect	1849	9	Lost election recount
3	Nathan Porter	1878	34	Died
4	Jonathan Dudley	1883	40	Lost election recount
5	Samuel Boring	1887	42	Term ended
6	John H. Harper	1852	54	Lost election recount
7	Eli Wright	1905	57	Expelled
8	Frederick Woodworth	1857	66	Term ended
9	John W. Bones	1877	70	Term ended
10	Alexander Anderson	1852	90	Resigned
11	Orrin Z. Hubbell	1903	103	Died
12	**Vanessa Delgado**	2018	110	Term ended
13	Michael J. Burns	1949	119	Died
14	Jesse W. Carter	1939	155	Term Ended
15	Harry I. Thornton	1861	164	Resigned
16	Clarence J. Tauzer	1948	188	Died
17	Jesse W. Carter	1939	237	Resigned
18	Clair Engle	1943	253	Resigned
19	Charles H. S. Williams	1859	277	Resigned
20	**Larry Stirling**	1989	299	Resigned
21	**Joe Baca**	1999	351	Resigned

---

[131] Names in **BOLD** indicate living former legislators.

County/Counties	Last Republican	Last Democrat	Last Elected
Sutter		Harold E. Booth	1962
Yuba		Paul J. Lunardi	1962
Nevada		Stephen P. Teale	1968
Lassen		Pauline L. Davis	1974
Modoc		Pauline L. Davis	1974
Plumas		Pauline L. Davis	1974
Sierra		Pauline L. Davis	1974
Siskiyou		Pauline L. Davis	1974
Humboldt		Peter H. Behr	1974
Mendocino		Peter H. Behr	1974
Inyo		Walter W. Stiern	1978
Solano	Don Sebastiani		1980
San Francisco	Milton Marks		1984
Butte		Mike Thompson	1990
Glenn		Mike Thompson	1990
Shasta		Mike Thompson	1990
Marin	Bill Filante		1990
Alpine		Patrick Johnston	1991
Calaveras		Patrick Johnston	1991
Mono		Patrick Johnston	1991
Mariposa		Margaret E. Snyder	1992
Tuolumne		Margaret E. Snyder	1992
San Mateo	Tom Campbell		1993
Lake	Maurice Johannessen		1998
Napa	Maurice Johannessen		1998
Sonoma	Maurice Johannessen		1998
Imperial	Bonnie Garcia		2006
Amador		Alyson Huber	2010
El Dorado		Alyson Huber	2010
Placer		Richard Pan	2010
Santa Clara	Sam Blakeslee		2010
Santa Cruz	Sam Blakeslee		2010
Yolo	Jim Nielsen		2010
Del Norte	Jim Nielsen		2013
Trinity	Jim Nielsen		2013
Kings	Andy Vidak		2014
Monterey	Anthony Cannella		2014
San Benito	Anthony Cannella		2014
Alameda	Catherine Baker		2016
Contra Costa	Catherine Baker		2016

Last Democrat from Yuba

"I come from a family of Democrats... they love America.. we will be fine."
- Senator Anthony Cannella[132]

Everybody knows that San Francisco doesn't usually elect Republicans, but did you know that it has been three decades since the last San Francisco Republican served in the Legislature?

Currently, sixteen counties are represented in Sacramento by legislators of both parties[133]. The two counties represented longest by only Republicans are Sutter and Yuba, both of which last had a Democratic state legislator nearly sixty years ago. As noted in an earlier chapter, Assemblywoman Pauline Davis, the last Democrat to represent Modoc, Plumas, Siskiyou, Lassen and Sierra counties, was also the only woman in the legislature between 1961 and 1966.

Another twenty-one counties are exclusively represented in the legislature by Democrats. The longest Democrat-only counties are Humboldt and Mendocino, which last elected a Republican in the 1970s.

The table to the left shows the final Democratic and Republican legislators from the single party counties, along with the year they were last elected. Since this table was last produced in the 2017 edition, a few counties changed hands. In 2018, Anna Caballero became the first Democratic legislator to represent Madera County since 2000 and Melissa Hurtado the first to represent Tulare County since 2010.

In 2020, Suzette Martinez Valladares became the first Republican to represent Ventura County in two years.

---

[132] Facebook post (@SenAnthonyCannella) 11/6/2018
https://www.facebook.com/SenAnthonyCannella/posts/2160928437271304
[133] These counties are Colusa, Fresno, Kern, Los Angeles, Madera, Orange, Riverside, Sacramento, San Bernardino, San Diego, San Joaquin, San Luis Obispo, Santa Barbara, Stanislaus, Tulare, and Ventura.

Most Votes for State Senate Candidates (1849-Present)[134]

	Candidate	Vote	Election
1	*Richard B. Richards (Dem.)*	*1,409,469*	*1958*
2	*Thomas M. Rees (Dem.)*	*1,167,285*	*1962*
3	*Jack B. Tenney (Rep.)*	*1,126,157*	*1950*
4	*Jack B. Tenney (Rep.)*	*833,565*	*1946*
5	*Richard B. Richards (Dem.)*	*786,823*	*1954*
6	*Jack B. Tenney (Dem.)*	*679,012*	*1942*
7	**Nancy Skinner (Dem.)**	**404,455**	**2020**
8	**Josh Becker (Dem.)**	**348,005**	**2020**
9	**Steve Glazer (Dem.)**	**339,925**	**2020**
10	**Toni G. Atkins (Dem.)**	**336,467**	**2020**
11	**Brian D. Dahle (Rep.)**	**326,836**	**2020**
12	**Bill Dodd (Dem.)**	**323,317**	**2020**
13	**John Laird (Dem.)**	**320,090**	**2020**
14	Mark Leno (Dem.)	303,241	2012
15	Loni Hancock (Dem.)	300,994	2012
16	Ben Allen (Dem.)	298,609	2018
17	Jerry Hill (Dem.)	296,400	2016
18	**Anthony Portantino (Dem.)**	**295,432**	**2020**
19	Ted Gaines (Rep.)	287,314	2016
20	**Henry Stern (Dem.)**	**284,797**	**2020**
21	*Nicholas C. Petris (Dem.)*	*283,179*	*1972*
22	Tom Torlakson (Dem.)	282,714	2004
23	**Monique Limon (Dem.)**	**272,442**	**2020**
24	Loni Hancock (Dem.)	272,225	2008
25	Joe Simitian (Dem.)	272,154	2008

---

[134] **Bold** indicates a record set in the 2020 General Election.
Italicized indicates deceased.

Most and Fewest Votes

Prior to the 1964 U.S. Supreme Court decision in Reynolds v. Sims, California's legislative districts had been drawn according to what was called the "Little Federal Model" in which Assembly districts were drawn according to population (like the U.S. House of Representatives) and the State Senate was drawn according to counties (similar to the U.S. Senate being divided by states).

The resulting Senate districts were massively different in population, which was reflected in the election results. For example, in the 1958 election, Richard B. Richards won in District 38 with 1.4 million votes while Charles Brown in District 28 won his with just 4,269. In fact, the massive 38th Senate District (which included all of Los Angeles County) gave us the six highest vote counts for legislators in state history.

Although modern legislative boundaries are redrawn each decade to equalize the number of residents in each districts, there can be a lot variation in population by the end of the ten years. Combine that with variation in the number of people eligible to vote (because of age or citizenship status) and different turnout rates for various types of elections and you'll see some significant variation in the number of votes that it takes to get elected.

Probably no election in modern history illustrated that better than the recent 2020 General election, in which Assembly candidates won with nine of the ten highest vote counts in state history and seven of the top ten post-1960s Senate vote totals. That's a lot of votes.

Most Votes for State Assembly Candidates (1849-Present) [135]

	Candidate	Votes	Date
1	**Buffy Wicks (Dem.)**	**204,108**	**2020**
2	**Rebecca Bauer-Kahan (Dem.)**	**192,977**	**2020**
3	**David Chiu (Dem.)**	**190,731**	**2020**
4	**Rob Bonta (Dem.)**	**190,168**	**2020**
5	Tony Thurmond (Dem.)	189,530	2016
6	**Mark W. Stone (Dem.)**	**185,496**	**2020**
7	**Kevin Mullin (Dem.)**	**182,419**	**2020**
8	**Kevin Kiley (Rep.)**	**178,559**	**2020**
9	**Jim Patterson (Rep.)**	**177,600**	**2020**
10	**Phil Ting (Dem.)**	**175,858**	**2020**
11	David Chiu (Dem.)	172,153	2016
12	Richard Bloom (Dem.)	167,428	2018
13	Ted Gaines (Rep.)	166,736	2008
14	**Evan Low (Dem.)**	**166,733**	**2020**
15	**Richard Bloom (Dem.)**	**166,503**	**2020**
16	**Steve Bennett (Dem.)**	**166,015**	**2020**
17	**Frank Bigelow (Rep.)**	**165,624**	**2020**
18	Nancy Skinner (Dem.)	164,929	2012
19	**Tim Grayson (Dem.)**	**163,205**	**2020**
20	Tom Ammiano (Dem.)	162,977	2008
21	Nancy Skinner (Dem.)	162,432	2008
22	**Jim Wood (Dem.)**	**162,287**	**2020**
23	**Laurie Davies (Rep.)**	**161,650**	**2020**
24	Tom Ammiano (Dem.)	161,124	2012
25	**Chris Holden (Dem.)**	**160,878**	**2020**

---

[135] **Bold** indicates a record set in the 2020 General Election.

Fewest Votes for Winning State Senate Candidates (by decade)

Decade	Senator	Votes	Year
1940s	Charles Brown (Dem.)	2,566	1946
1950s	Stephen P. Teale (Dem.)	2,100	1953
1960s	William Symons Jr. (Rep.)	3,525	1962
1970s	Dennis E. Carpenter (Rep.)	22,074	1970
1980s	John Seymour (Rep.)	30,856	1982
1990s	Charles M. Calderon (Dem.)	22,857	1990
2000s	Gloria Romero (Dem.)	26,959	2001
2010s	Isadore Hall[136] (Dem.)	17,951	2014
2020s	Melissa Melendez (Rep.)	105,940	2020

Fewest Votes for Winning State Assembly Candidates (by decade)

Decade	Assemblymember	Votes	Year
1940s	George Roy Butters (Rep.)	6,287	1946
1950s	George A. Willson (Write-in)	905	1958
1960s	Victor V. Veysey (Rep.)	9,464	1962
1970s	Teresa P. Hughes (Dem.)	7,230	1975
1980s	Lucille Roybal-Allard (Dem.)	5,541	1987
1990s	Denise M. Ducheny (Dem.)	5,150	1994
2000s	Felipe Fuentes (Dem.)	5,819	2007
2010s	Freddie Rodriguez (Dem.)	7,630	2013
2020s	Rudy Salas (Dem.)	63,450	2020

---

[136] Isadore Hall was elected to the Senate in 2014 with a remarkably low number of votes. His victory was won with fewer votes than any other candidate since Fred Marler in 1965.

Constitution of the
State of California
and of the
United States
and other Documents

Constitutional Amendments

Hanging on a wall in a hallway running to the rear of the Senate Chambers is a copy of Senate Joint Resolution 1 of 1865. The resolution was used by the California legislature to ratify the 13th Amendment banning slavery. Passed in the aftermath of the Civil War and assassination of President Lincoln, the resolution had broad support in California, which had been admitted to the Union as a free state.

Below the many rows of signatures by legislators who voted in support of the resolution are those of the fifteen (eleven Assemblymembers and four senators) who voted no. Of the fifteen no votes, fourteen never held another political office. It's a good reminder of the importance of the historic choices that lawmakers face as well as of the consequences of a vote cast out of step with the district's voters.

Compared to the frequent attempts to amend the State Constitution[137], the U.S. Constitution has been amended only twice in the last fifty years. An important, although rarely exercised responsibility of state legislatures is the ratification of federal constitutional amendments. As you may recall from high school government class, amendments to the U.S. Constitution are proposed by Congress and then must be affirmed by two thirds of the state legislatures to be enacted.

Fourteen amendments to the U.S. Constitution have been ratified since California became a state. Thirteen were ratified by the legislature and one by a special state convention authorized by statute. Another, the 15th Amendment, received its approval by California almost eighty years after it became law.

---

[137] There were 205 amendments to the state constitution proposed in the past decade according to the LegInfo website [http://leginfo.legislature.ca.gov/].

In 1869, as the U.S. struggled with the reconstruction and establishment of fair voting laws in the Southern states, Congress proposed the following amendment:

> *Section 1. The right of citizens of the United States to vote shall not be denied or abridged by the United States or by any State on account of race, color, or previous condition of servitude.*
>
> *Section 2. The Congress shall have power to enforce this article by appropriate legislation.*

When California's legislature reconvened in 1870, State Senator John S. Hager[138] introduced Senate Joint Resolution 3 (SJR 3) which declared California's opposition to the law and affirmatively rejected the amendment. The legislature moved quickly, with both houses overwhelmingly approving the resolution in just two days. In spite of California's opposition, the amendment was approved by enough states to become law on March 30, 1870.

Ninety-two years later, the California legislature took its second vote on the amendment. State Senator Al Rodda, who had been a history teacher before being elected to the legislature, introduced SJR 9 in 1962. Not surprisingly, the resolution passed both houses in just four days without a single no vote.

California has never ratified the first twelve amendments to the U.S. Constitution and while it's not legally unnecessary (it wouldn't impact the legality of those parts of the Constitution), it might not be a bad bill idea.

---

[138] Three years later, Hager would become one of California's U.S. Senators, serving December 23, 1873 to March 3, 1875.

California Ratification of Federal Constitutional Amendments

The **1ˢᵗ - 12ᵗʰ Amendments** were ratified between 1791 and 1804, more than forty years before California became a state. They have never been ratified by the State of California.

The **13ᵗʰ Amendment**, relating to slavery and involuntary servitude, was ratified by SJR 1 (1865) introduced by State Senator William J. Shaw. The resolution passed the Senate 35-4 and the Assembly 66-11.

The **14ᵗʰ Amendment**, relating to the rights of citizenship and equal protection, was ratified by AJR 32 (1959) introduced by Assemblymen Bruce F. Allen and John C. Williamson. The resolution passed the Senate 29-0 and the Assembly 66-0.

The **15ᵗʰ Amendment**, relating to the right to vote, was first voted on in 1870, when SJR 3 (1870) by State Senator John S. Hager affirmatively rejected the amendment. The Senate rejected the amendment by a vote of 23-8 and the Assembly concurred 57-8. The 15ᵗʰ Amendment became law without California's ratification on March 30, 1870. Ninety-two years later, the 15ᵗʰ Amendment was ratified by SJR 9 (1962) introduced by State Senator Albert S. Rodda. The resolution passed the Senate 31-0 and the Assembly 66-0.

The **16ᵗʰ Amendment**, permitting the collection of an income tax, was ratified by SJR 2 (1911) introduced by State Senator John B. Sanford. The resolution passed the Senate 33-0 and was adopted by the Assembly on a voice roll call.

The **17ᵗʰ Amendment**, relating to the popular election of U.S. Senators, was ratified by AJR 5 (1913) introduced by the Assembly Committee on Federal Relations. The resolution passed the Senate 34-0 and the Assembly 67-0.

The **18ᵗʰ Amendment**, banning the manufacture, sale, or transportation of liquor, was ratified by SJR 4 (1919) introduced by State Senator Samuel Cary Evans, Jr. The resolution passed the Senate 25-14 and the Assembly 48-28.

The **19th Amendment**, establishing women's suffrage nationwide, was ratified by SJR 1x1 (1919) introduced by State Senator S. C. Evans. The resolution passed the Senate 39-0 and the Assembly 73-2.

The **20th Amendment**, relating to the terms of Presidents, Vice Presidents, and Congress, was ratified by AJR 1 (1933) introduced by Assemblyman Ernest Crowley, B.J. Feigenbaum and Ray D. Williamson. The resolution passed the Senate 40-0 and the Assembly 71-0.

The **21st Amendment**, which repealed the 18th Amendment and legalized the manufacture, sale, or transportation of liquor, was ratified on July 24, 1933 at a State Convention authorized by AB 2316 (1933). A total of 13 legislators (twelve Assemblymembers and one Senator) voted against AB 2316 (1933) while it was before the legislature.

The **22nd Amendment**, establishing term limits for Presidents, was ratified by SJR 16 (1947) introduced by State Senator George J. Hatfield and 26 coauthors. The resolution passed the Senate 27-10 and the Assembly 45-30.

The **23rd Amendment**, which permitted the District of Columbia to elect Presidential Electors, was ratified by AJR 4 (1961) introduced by Assemblyman Phil Burton and 55 coauthors. The resolution passed the Senate 26-0 and the Assembly 61-13.

The **24th Amendment**, ending the use of poll taxes, was ratified by SJR 1 (1963) introduced by Senator John Holmdahl. The resolution passed the Senate 33-0 and the Assembly 70-3.

The **25th Amendment**, relating to the removal of the President, was ratified by AJR 2x1 (1965) introduced by Assembly Speaker Jesse Unruh. The resolution passed the Senate 32-5 and the Assembly 66-1.

The **26th Amendment**, lowering the minimum voting age from twenty-one to eighteen years, was ratified by SJR 22 (1971) introduced by State Senator Mervyn M. Dymally. The resolution passed the Senate 22-12 and the Assembly 52-14.

The **27th Amendment**, limiting Congressional pay raises, was ratified by SJR 1 (1992) introduced by State Senator Quentin Kopp. The resolution passed the Senate 33-0 and the Assembly 75-0.

California's Codes

"The making of laws is something like the breeding of rabbits; you buy yourself a couple of rabbits, and the next thing you know, you have a yard full, and your wife is beginning to complain about a number of things, including the smell..."[139]
- *Senator John R. Phillips*

For the first twenty years California was a state, its laws were organized only by the order that they were signed into law. This lack of organized laws made record-keeping much easier for a legislature that was constantly on the move, but made it very difficult to find related laws or identify laws that had been repealed or amended.

In the late 1860s, the Legislature created a Code Commission and Creed Haymond, a brilliant attorney for the Southern Pacific Railroad, was appointed to fill one of the three positions. In his work representing the railroad, Creed Haymond had been working for years on the complicated work of tracking the creation of new statutes, the conflicts between existing laws, and the removal of laws that had been superseded by later laws.

Although just one of several commissioners, he was seen as the most active participant. California's laws were divided into four codes; Political, Civil, Penal, and the Code of Civil Procedure. The largest of these was the Political Code, which has since been divided into nearly all of the newer codes that we have today.

It was 50 years before the need was felt to divide California law into additional codes; the Probate Code would become California's fifth in 1931. The creation of the Probate Code started a rush of new code creation to segregate the increasingly complicated laws of California into bite-sized pieces. By the end of the 1930s, an additional sixteen new

---

[139] Inside California by Senator John Phillips (Murray & Gee; 1939), pages 19-20.

codes had been organized. The quick pace was halted by the outbreak of World War II, and although it continued after, it was at a far slower rate.

As of today, only two new codes have been created in the past fifty years, and the most recent was nearly three decades ago. It appears that the division of California laws is complete.

Code	Created	Author
Penal Code	1871	Code Commission
Political Code	1871	Code Commission
Civil Code	1871	Code Commission
Code of Civil Procedure	1871	Code Commission
Probate Code	1931	Herbert C. Jones, H. C. Nelson, and George W. Rochester
Military Code	1933	Roy J. Nielsen
School Code	1933	Ford A. Chatters
Agriculture Code	1933	Herbert W. Slater
Fish and Game Code	1933	Hubert B. Scudder
Insurance Code	1935	Dan E. Williams
Military and Veterans Code	1935	Roy J. Nielsen
Streets and Highways Code	1935	Nelson T. Edwards
Vehicle Code	1935	William B. Hornblower
Labor Code	1937	Thomas A. Maloney

Code	Created	Author
Harbors and Navigation Code	1937	Roy J. Nielsen
Welfare and Institutions Code	1937	Andrew Schottky
Business and Professions Code	1937	Chester M. Gannon
Revenue and Taxation Code	1939	Gardiner Johnson and George P. Miller
Elections Code	1939	Jeanette E. Daley
Public Resources Code	1939	Hubert B. Scudder
Health and Safety Code	1939	Frank W. Mixter and John D. Foley
Government Code	1943	Edward Fletcher and Hugh Burns
Education Code	1943	Herbert W. Slater
Water Code	1943	Randolph Collier and Oliver J. Carter
Corporations Code	1947	M. Philip Davis
Public Utilities Code	1951	Jess R. Dorsey
Unemployment Insurance Code	1953	Ernest R. Geddes
Commercial Code	1963	Fred Farr
Evidence Code	1965	Alfred Song
Financial Code	1969	John T. Knox
Food and Agricultural Code	1969	Howard Way
Public Contract Code	1981	Elihu Harris
Family Code	1992	Jackie Speier

Mason's Big Idea

Imagine being incredibly gifted at bringing information from different sources together in a way that makes perfect sense. Would you become a police detective, interviewing witnesses with conflicting stories in order to solve complicated crimes? Would you become an investor, analyzing corporate financials to find the best companies to invest in? When Paul Mason had this gift and applied it to his work in the California legislature, he designed the system that runs a majority of state legislatures in the United States today.

Mason, who served as the Deputy Secretary of the Senate, is probably best described as someone who liked to understand the way things worked. Likely inspired by a series of books[140] written about California's Progressive era, Mason wrote his Master's thesis describing the complicated way in which state laws, the rules of the legislature, and court decisions worked together to dictate how legislatures meet and make laws. In his paper, titled "Procedure in the California Legislature," he combined an internal handbook explaining legislative procedures with books written to explain to the public the ways coalitions form to support or oppose legislation.

He was drawn to Sacramento and the following year Mason took a seat in the front row as Minute Clerk and File Clerk for the State Senate. Over the next few years, he moved quickly up the ranks of legislative staff until he was elected Chief Assistant Secretary of the Senate in 1929.

Similar to the work done by Creed Haymond in organizing the laws of California into codes in the 1860s (see "California's Codes" on page 125), Mason began painstakingly compiling the text of the State Constitution, starting with the original text approved by voters in 1879 and updating it amendment by amendment. In two years of heavy research, during

---

[140] Franklin Hichborn's series of books titled <u>The Story of the Session of the California Legislature</u> covered in minute detail the actions of the legislature in 1909, 1911, 1913, 1915 and 1921.

which he discovered "a forgotten constitutional amendment" that had been overlooked years before[141], Mason had completed his first major work. Even today, virtually any version of the Constitution that you're likely to encounter (in books printed by the state or online databases run by private legal research companies) shares a lineage including Mason's 1933 edition.

Almost immediately, Mason pivoted to an even more ambitious project - writing a complete manual of legislative procedure. This required Mason to compile parts of the Constitution, state law, the rules of the two houses, various court decisions, and hundreds of years of parliamentary traditions. He then had to work out which law took precedence and note the source and explanation.

Two years later, on January 31st, 1935, newspapers reported that Mason had completed work on "the only complete legislative manual ever written." The book, which filled nearly 400 pages in a type-written draft, was hailed as a model to be used by state legislatures nationwide. That prediction has largely been fulfilled and, as of 2021, the National Conference of State Legislatures notes that 70 of the 99 legislative chambers in the United States use Mason's Manual.

The most recent edition of Mason's Manual was released in 2020 and it stretches for 852 pages.

---

[141] "California News Review" Lompoc Review, Volume XIII, Number 10, 28 July 1931. Page 6.

The Tie-Breaker

One of California's rarest legislative actions, the casting vote, has only been used three times in the past fifty years. As the President of the Senate, the California State Constitution gives the Lieutenant Governor the ability to use a "casting vote" to break a tie vote in the upper house. This is a good reminder of an earlier time when the Lieutenant Governor was a more active participant in the life of the Senate.

With only a few exceptions, Senators were assigned to their committees by the President of the Senate until 1939[142]. The casting vote may not be used on two-thirds vote bills (urgency bills or constitutional amendments) and may not be used if the vote ties with less than all Senators voting.

The first casting vote in California history was on December 18, 1849 (on only the third day of the first session)[143]. During the adoption of the Senate Rules, Senator John Bidwell proposed that each rule be voted on individually. When the vote tied 6 to 6, the Senate President[144] broke the tie by voting no.

Casting Votes in the State Senate (1971-2021)

Date	Lt. Governor	Bill	Author	Casting Vote
8/20/1996	Gray Davis	AB 1982	Pete Knight	NO
8/25/1976	Mervyn Dymally	AB 1713	Floyd Mori	AYE
5/1/1976	Mervyn Dymally	AB 489	Willie Brown	AYE

---

[142] Legislature of California by C.C. Young (Commonwealth Club; 1943), page 256.
[143] Journal of the Senate of the State of California at the First Session, page 11.
[144] Because on December 18th the Senate had only twelve members and the first Lt. Governor wouldn't be sworn into office until Thursday, this casting vote was made by the President pro Tempore.

Veto Override

When a bill sails through the legislature with broad bipartisan support only to be vetoed by the Governor, thoughts almost without fail turn to the veto override. After all, what could be more satisfying for the author of a vetoed bill than possibility of brushing the Governor aside and forcing the bill into law?

Although veto-overrides are threatened on occasion, it has been nearly 40 years since the legislature exercised this ability. The primary reason is that veto-overrides are seen as a significant insult to the Governor and major disruption to the balance of power relationship between the three branches.

In the last 75 years, only six bills have had their vetoes overturned by the legislature. In his ten years in office, Earl Warren had only one veto overridden. Governor Reagan had a single override in his eight years leading the state. In his first two terms in office, Jerry Brown had a total of four vetoes overridden (in 1977 and 1979).

"Recent" Overrides of Governors' Vetoes

Year	Governor	Majority Party (Senate/Assembly)	Veto Overrides
1979	Jerry Brown (D)	Democrat / Democrat	3
1977	Jerry Brown (D)	Democrat / Democrat	1
1974	Ronald Reagan (R)	Democrat / Democrat	1
1946	Earl Warren (R)	Republican / Republican	1
1941	Culbert Olson (D)	Republican / Democrat	8
1939	Culbert Olson (D)	Republican / Democrat	3
1933	James Rolph (R)	Republican / Republican	17

Assemblywoman Autumn Burke (Class of 2014) with her mother former Assemblywoman Yvonne Brathwaite Burke (Class of 1967).

Legislative Classes

"It seems but a brief time ago when I first took my oath of office, full of apprehension and scared clear down to the socks. Would I make the grade, would I be worthy of the public trust and would I be worthy of the respect of the various members? I suppose to almost all of us, that has been our experience."
- Assemblyman Don A. Allen[145]

In the past century, there have been 1,332 new members elected to California Legislature, of whom 559 are still alive[146]. With so many individuals, it can be challenging to find useful ways to divide the group. One of the best is by grouping legislators according to the first legislative session they served in.

Regardless of political party, new legislators face many similar challenges as they first arrive in Sacramento, from preparing their families for the long absences that will become routine to hiring their new staff and learning about the committees to which they've been assigned. Even after leaving office, members who arrived together often celebrate milestones with reunions[147].

The large incoming classes, like those of 1967 and 2012, frequently reflect significant changes to the rules by which legislators are elected. In the

---

[145] Don A. Allen, Sr. Letter to Nelson S. Dilworth. 18 June 1959. From the Dilworth Collection.

[146] This number, current as of December 31, 2020, includes current and former members. The author is grateful to Paul Mitchell of Political Data Inc. for providing valuable assistance in the effort to identify and locate seven decades of former legislators.

[147] One of my favorite stories is of the seven surviving members of the Assembly Class of 1961, who celebrated their 20th anniversary by signing a contract to entrust a case of brandy with a longtime lobbyist and pledging that they would all meet and share a bottle each time one died. The plan worked for decades until, after the death of the lobbyist, it was discovered that he had drunk all the remaining brandy several years before.

case of 1967 and 2012, the changes were to the process by which the Senate districts were drawn and, in the second, in how term limits work. At the other end of the spectrum is the Class of 1984, with only five members, which stands out as the smallest in state history.

This guide to the incoming classes of legislators begins with 1961, the earliest class with a living member.

The charts on the following pages contain lines representing four dates in the life of each legislator. For simplicity, only four dates in each legislator's life are represented; birth, death, and the start and end of their legislative service. This may cause some confusion in the cases of the five percent of legislators who have a break in service of more than a year, but it effectively communicates the relative service of most members.

The Lives of Five Legislators

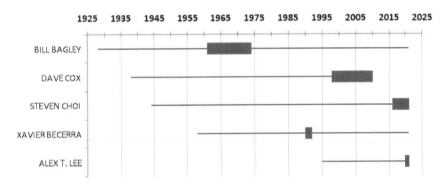

Five columns representing the lives and time in office of
Bill Bagley, Dave Cox, Steven Choi, Xavier Becerra, and Alex T. Lee.

The charts on the following pages contain lines representing four dates in the life of each legislator. In each column, there is a *thin line* that charts their life and a **thick line** that represents their time in office.

- The *thin line* begins in the year of their birth and extends until their death (if they have died) or the present (if they're still alive).

- The **thick line** identifies the portion of their life between when they first assumed office and when they left the legislature. This chart does not depict breaks in service for individuals who left office and later returned to the legislature.

The chart on the previous page plots the lives of five legislators; Bill Bagley, Dave Cox, Steven Choi, Xavier Becerra, and Alex T. Lee.

The first line represents the life of Assemblyman Bill Bagley. The thin line representing his life begins with his birth in 1928 and continues to the present. The thick portion signifies his time in office (between 1961 and 1974). Bagley has been a former legislator for 47 years, which is represented by the thin line from 1974 to the present.

The second line represents Senator Dave Cox. Cox was born in 1938 and served in the legislature from 1998 until his death in 2010. Because Senator Cox died in office, he has no thin line representing life after leaving office.

The third represents Assemblyman Steven Choi, the oldest freshman Assemblyman since the end of World War II. Because he remains in office today, he too has no line representing life after office.

The fourth traces the life of U.S. Senator Xavier Becerra, who was born in 1958, and served a single term in the Assembly from 1991 to 1992 before leaving to become a member of Congress.

The final line represents Alex T. Lee, the youngest legislator since the 1930s. He was born in 1995 and began his first term in December 2020.

NOTE: Absences

California Lawmaker

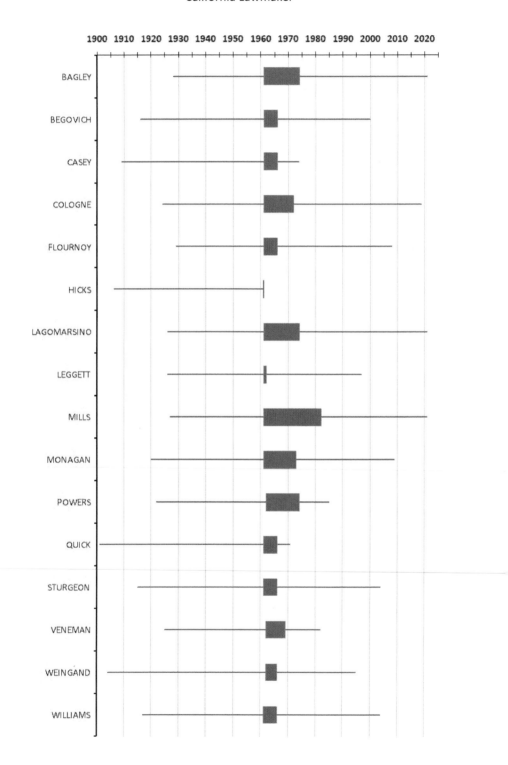

Class of 1961

As my friend Bill Bagley loves to remind me every time we talk, this was a great class. The newcomers in 1961 included future State Controller Hugh Flournoy and Bob Monagan. Monagan remains the only Republican since the late 1950s to serve as Speaker for a full-term[148]. After leaving office, he wrote a book[149] about his experiences, in which he offered his "Monagan's Laws" about government including;

"Campaign expenditures rise to meet campaign contributions."

Another author from this class who would both lead a house and write a book was James R. Mills, who served as Senate President Pro Tem between 1971 and 1981. Mills' book, about the time he spent in the Assembly, is one of the best first-person accounts of the legislature in the 1960s including the hubris and ultimate downfall of Speaker Jesse Unruh[150]. Thirty years after being published, Mills' book remains strongly recommended reading for all new legislators and staff.

A third member of the class, Bill Bagley, wrote his own book to tell tales of old friends and explain his thoughts on what made government work so well during California's "golden years". In fact, when he eventually wrote to his own book, this was the title he gave it[151].

In an interesting intersection with national politics, Senator Alvin C Wiegand of Santa Barbara, elected in a 1962 special election, owned and operated the San Ysidro Ranch from the 1930s to the 1970s. The San Ysidro, a resort that opened in the 1890s, is where John and Jacqueline Kennedy honeymooned after their 1953 marriage.

---

[148] Three Republicans were Speaker for a total of 18 months during 1995-1996.
[149] The Disappearance of Representative Government by Robert T. Monagan (Comstock Bonanza Press; 1990)
[150] A Disorderly House: The Brown-Unruh Years in Sacramento (Heyday Books; 1987)
[151] California's Golden Years: When Government Worked and Why (IGS Press; 2009)

California Lawmaker

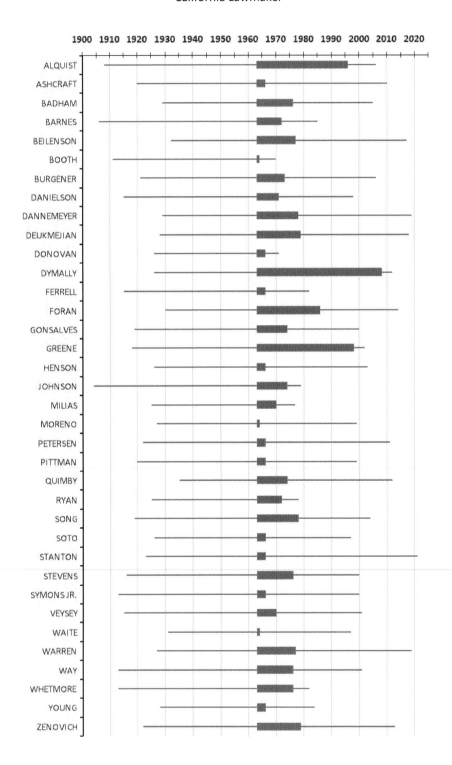

Class of 1963

The Class of 1963 was one that would change the state. It had the very first legislators who were born in the 1930s; John F. Foran (born 1930), Tom Waite (born 1931), Tony Beilenson[152] (born 1932) and John P. Quimby (born 1935). The class had seven members elected to Congress, a record that still stands today.

Two members of this class would become state constitutional officers; Governor George Deukmejian and Lt. Governor Mervyn Dymally. Dymally's amazingly long career including four years in the Assembly and twelve in the Senate[153] before being elected Lieutenant Governor in 1974. After eight years as Lieutenant Governor, he was elected to Congress, where he served six terms. Not quite done, Dymally returned to the Assembly from 2002 to 2008.

This was the first class since 1937 that didn't have a member die in office as a state legislator, although one died in Congress. During his time in Sacramento, Leo Ryan suggested that the Assembly adopt an official seal, which remains in use today[154].

Several years after being elected to Congress, Ryan was asked to investigate the welfare of some of his former constituents who had been moved to South America by cult leader Jim Jones. Arriving at the compound, some of the people Ryan met told him that they were being held against their will. Congressman Ryan began an evacuation of all who wanted to leave, but was killed when the escaping group was attacked by cult loyalists.

---

[152] After retiring from Congress, Beilenson discovered a journal that he had written during his time in the State Senate. He published Sacramento Diaries (2004) with only grammatical changes, providing some of the most frank and open insights into the thoughts and private conversations of a legislator.

[153] Dymally was the first African American to serve in the State Senate.

[154] Ryan left a second contribution to the institution as the author of Understanding California Government and Politics (Fearon Publishers; 1966) in which he describes life as a legislator and humorously explains the unending confusion about what exactly it is that Assemblymen assemble.

California Lawmaker

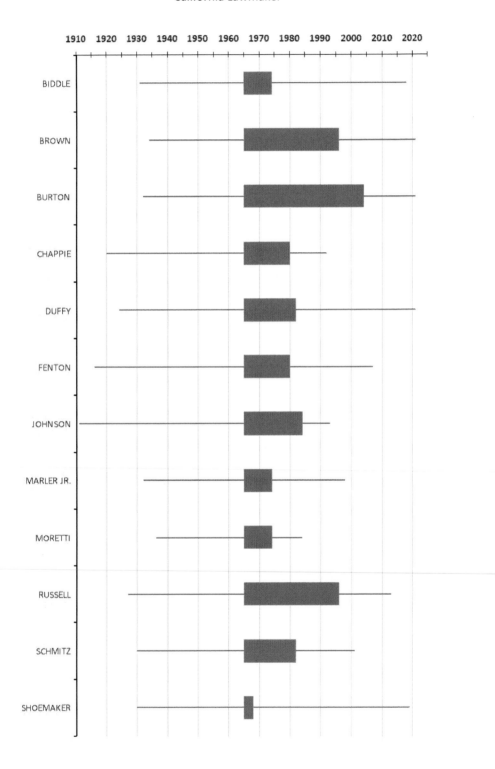

Class of 1965

For a relatively small class (just twelve members), the Class of 1965 had a huge impact on California. The four youngest members of the class included two Assembly Speakers[155] (including the longest-serving Speaker in state history), a Senate President pro Tem, and a Senate Minority Leader. The other members included two Assembly Majority Leaders (Biddle and Fenton) and a Presidential candidate (Schmitz).

Bob Moretti, who became a member at age 28, became Speaker in 1971. He resigned as Speaker after declining reelection to instead run an unsuccessful campaign for Governor in 1974[156]. Moretti's classmate Willie Brown won the Speakership in 1981 and held it for 15 years, establishing himself as the most powerful Speaker in state history. In a parallel to Jesse Unruh in the 1960s, Brown held onto the office through a declining caucus until the Republicans were able to seize control.

John Burton was elected to Congress in 1974, and served there until 1980, when he returned to the State Assembly. In 1996, after the session that saw the departure of Speaker Brown from the legislature, Burton moved to the State Senate. As Senate President pro Tem from 1998 to 2004, Burton created the model that is often imitated but has yet to be successfully duplicated.

The Class of 1965 also brought in Fred W. Marler, who at age 32 was the youngest Senator since 1950. By 1971, he had earned the respect of his Republican colleagues enough to be elected Senate Minority Leader. He served through 1974, when he left the legislature to become a judge for the Sacramento Superior Court. In 1987, he was elevated to California's Third District Court of Appeal.

---

[155] The all-time record was the Class of 1862, which included four future Speakers, Governor William Irwin, and Lt. Governor Timothy N. Machin.

[156] Speaker Moretti lost the 1974 election to Secretary of State Jerry Brown.

California Lawmaker

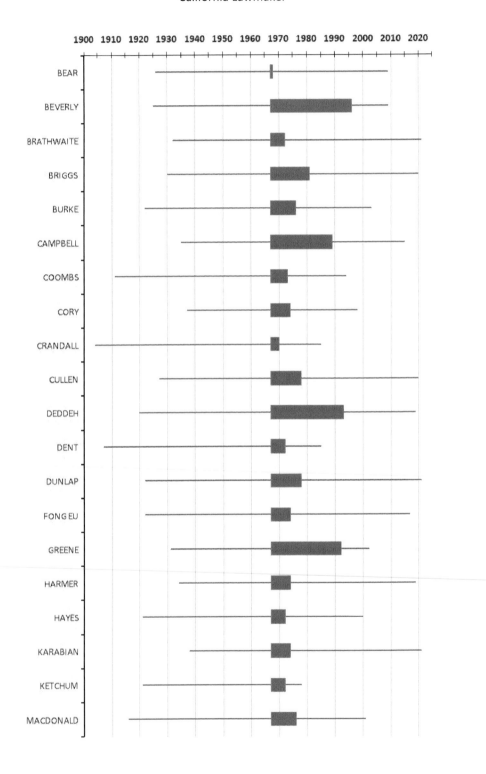

Class of 1967

The most accurate way to describe the 1966 election is to compare it to a tsunami. Like the massive wave, the election was set in motion by an earlier event and it would leave a lasting mark on the both legislature and state as a whole.

In 1964, the U.S. Supreme Court ruled[157] that the Equal Protection Clause of the U.S. Constitution required state legislative districts be roughly equal in population[158]. The ruling came as a shock in California, where Los Angeles County had been limited to a single Senate seat since 1911.

Of the twenty State Senators who were up for reelection in 1966, only one returned in 1967 (nine skipped reelection and retired, nine ran for reelection and were defeated, and one left to run for Congress). The Assembly had eighteen members leave as well, making it the largest turnover of legislators in a more than generation[159].

The class that arrived included four state constitutional officers; Governor Pete Wilson, Lt. Governor John L. Harmer, Secretary of State March Fong Eu, and State Controller Ken Cory. In a book he wrote while in the Senate, Harmer noted the importance of considering intrusion into personal lives when creating government programs, noting

> *"Erosion of freedom can be a subtle thing. The most innocent appearing and well-intentioned programs can become a means for destroying freedom or centralizing power in dangerous places."*[160]

Assemblymembers Earle Crandall and James W. Dent, the final two new legislators born in the 1900s, were members of this class. Among the younger members of the class were former NFL player Peter

---

[157] Reynolds v. Sims, 377 U.S. 533 (1964)

[158] See "Most and Fewest Votes" on page 115.

[159] In the Assembly, six incumbents ran again but were defeated, four left to become judges, one became State Controller, one went to Congress, and six declined reelection (including one who left to study poetry).

[160] We Dare Not Fail (Southwest Publishing Company; 1968)

California Lawmaker

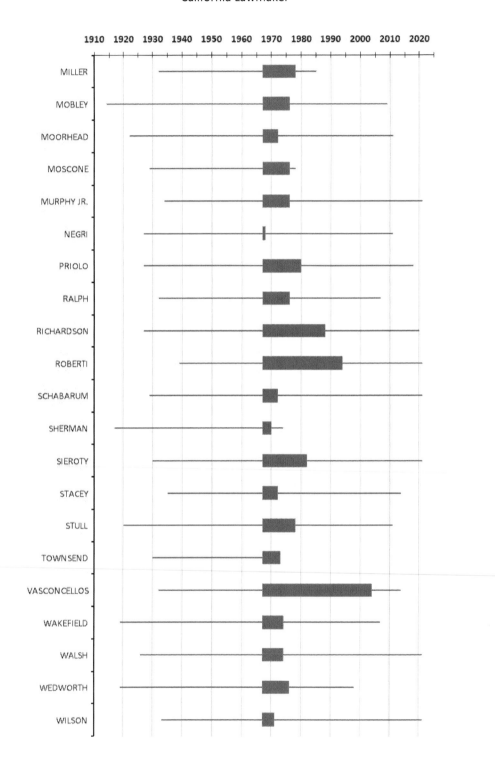

Schabarum of the San Francisco 49ers and John Vasconcellos, who had previously been Governor Pat Brown's "travel secretary" (he drove the Governor's car). Vasconcellos would go on to become a major proponent of self-esteem in the 1980s. This class also included the only fourth-generation legislator, Senator John F. Dunlap, whose uncle, grandfather, and great-grandfather had served in the legislature starting in the 1850s.

Senate leadership in this class included Senate President pro Tem David Roberti and Senate Majority Leader George Moscone. Roberti served as Senate President pro Tem for 14 years from 1980 to 1994, and is the only person in California history to continue holding a legislative leadership position for years after resigning[161]. Unfortunately for Roberti, it was because of this move that Roberti was the first legislator to be effected by term limits.

Senator H. L. Richardson was one of the most prolific writers to serve in the legislature in several decades. His first book, *Slightly to the Right!* was released the year he was elected to the Senate. He followed up with *Political Salt* in 1975 and *What Makes You Think We Read the Bills?* in 1978. In each of his books, Richardson told humorous stories about life in the Capitol and why things are the way they are.

In one part of *What Makes You Think We Read the Bills?*, Richardson explains the title of the book,

> *"People make a lot of assumptions about their representatives. One of the biggest is that legislators read the bills... Anyone who has ever read a bill can understand why the legislators hire staff to explain, or as we say, analyze and research, the legislation."*

It was true in the 1970s and is even truer today.

---

[161] It's a technicality... Roberti resigned from the Senate on July 2, 1992 in order to change seats. Due to the 1991 redistricting, Roberti was elected to a new term in SD-20 while only halfway through his term in SD-23.

California Lawmaker

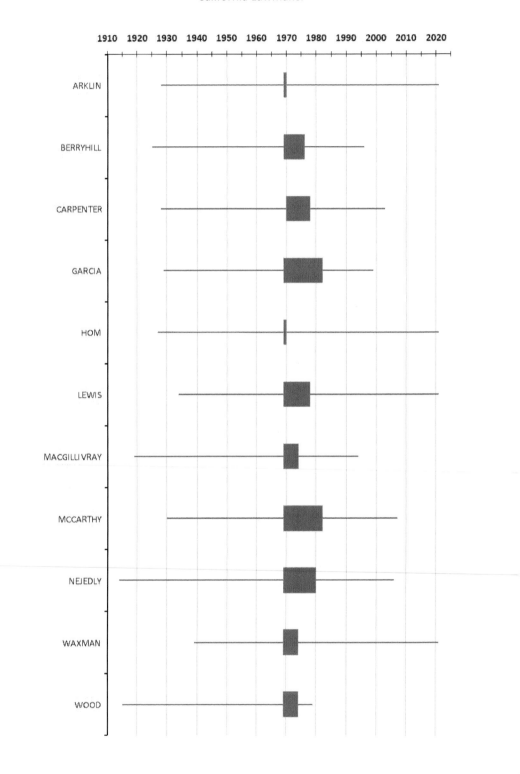

Class of 1969

For a class of legislators from over fifty years ago, there are a surprising number of familiar names in this group. The two youngest members of the class, Henry Waxman and Jerry Lewis, would be elected to Congress. Waxman served in Congress until 2015, Jerry Lewis retired in 2013. The third-youngest member of the class, Leo T. McCarthy, would serve as the presiding officer in both houses of the legislature, as Assembly Speaker (1974-1980), and as the longest-serving Lt. Governor in state history (1983-1995).

Clare Berryhill was elected to the Assembly in a 1969 special election, narrowly defeating Democrat Ernest LaCoste. In 1970, LaCoste would return the favor, beating Berryhill by two percent. Two years after that, the two would face each other a third time when the local Senate district became available.

Once again, Berryhill won and once again it was by a margin of less than a percent. The Berryhills are well acquainted with close elections. Clare's son Tom Berryhill narrowly lost an Assembly seat in 1996 by less than a hundred votes. Like his father, Tom would later serve in both the Assembly and Senate. Another son of Clare, Bill Berryhill, served two terms in the Assembly before losing yet another razor-close election for the Senate[162].

Alex P. Garcia, who served in the legislature until losing a reelection bid in 1982, served his constituents at a very dangerous time. In 1977, Senator Garcia assigned staff to investigate a halfway house that his office had received complaints about. One of Garcia's staffers, Robert Mark Lewis, became the most recent California legislative staffer to be assassinated when he was targeted by members of the Mexican Mafia gang.

---

[162] Tom and Bill Berryhill served in the Assembly together from 2008 to 2010, the first siblings to serve in the same house since Jack and Robert McCarthy served in the Senate together in 1955-1958.

California Lawmaker

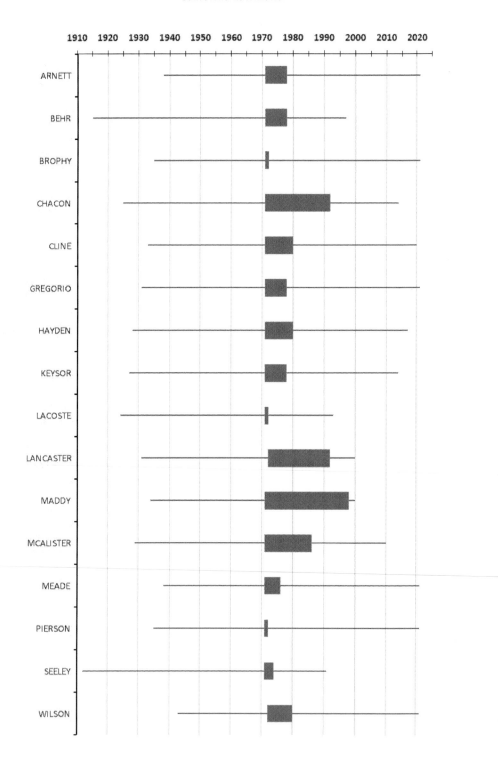

Class of 1971

Only two members of this class have served in both houses of the legislature; Bob Wilson and Ken Maddy. Maddy, the longest-serving member of the class, was also the only member of the class to attain a legislative leadership position (he served as Senate Minority Leader from 1987 to 1995).

Bill Brophy, the shortest-serving member of this class, served 414 days between a special election and the end of the term. In many ways, Brophy's time in office was like a shooting star that terrified onlookers and scorched everyone in the area. He survived a drive-by shooting of his house two days before the election and he was haunted for the duration of his term by some of worst luck and bad decisions that you can imagine.

Two of the nicest former legislators I have ever met, Alister McAlister and Richard D. Hayden, were members of this class. McAlister, who had been a law professor before his election to the Assembly, understood the importance of being a lawmaker. He authored more than 400 laws during his time in office, including a classic[163] that prevents property owners from being held liable for injuries that burglars receive while committing a burglary. Among the members who served with him, McAlister had the reputation as a "good guy" who was exceptionally honest.

Richard Hayden, a WWII veteran who served for a decade, is best remembered for securing the funding to create Mission College in Santa Clara. When he left the legislature in 1980, he was offered the job as President of the new college but declined, instead asking that he be allowed to occasionally teach introductory Political Science classes. He was still teaching thirty years later.

---

[163] In retrospect, it's hard to believe that nobody had thought of AB 200 (1985) before.

California Lawmaker

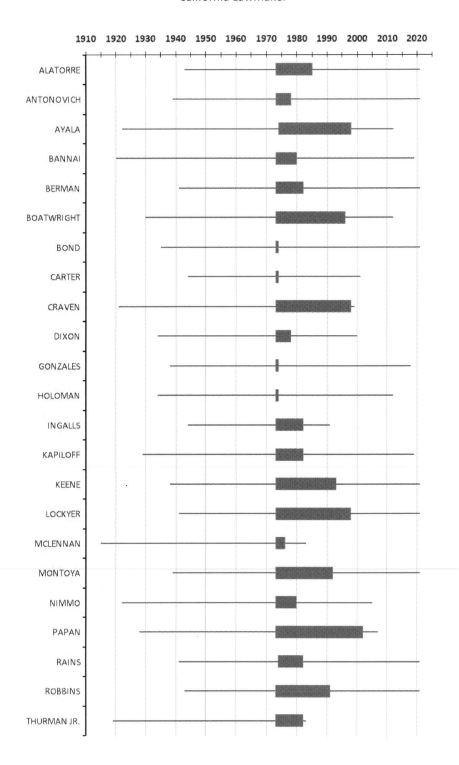

Class of 1973

This class included one state constitutional officer, Attorney General (and Treasurer) Bill Lockyer. Two members would go on to Congress, including 15-term Congressman Howard Berman and Julian C. Dixon, who died during his 11th term. It also had the very first freshman legislator who had been born in the 1940s; Bob Wilson (born 1943) would serve almost five years in the Assembly and another four in the Senate.

Lockyer, who was elected in a 1973 special election, would hold office continuously until 2014 and become the first person to term out of both houses and two statewide offices[164]. Mike Antonovich served six years in the Assembly followed by 36 years on the Los Angeles County Board of Supervisors. Antonovich ran for State Senate in 2016 and, had he been elected, his 38-year absence would have been the longest gap in state history.[165]

Joseph B. Montoya served in the legislature until 1990, when the FBI's Shrimpscam investigation ended his political career with convictions on seven corruption charges. Now a Sacramento resident, Montoya maintains that his conviction was a result of prosecutorial misconduct and he told me recently that he is working on an autobiography.

During an interview, Montoya described his class as "an interesting, diverse and mostly very aggressive bunch" with the exception of John Thurman, who was "the friendliest farmer I had ever met" and Paul Bannai who was "a gentle soul who had to be defeated simply because he was a Republican."

---

[164] The only other three people to serve in both houses of the legislature and in two statewide offices were Governors Frank Merriam, George Deukmejian, and Lt. Governor John Garamendi.

[165] Seventeen legislators have had a gap in service (or multiple gaps) of 20 years or longer. The longest was Assemblyman Frederick Lux, who had 37 years between his third term in 1865 and his fourth in 1903.

California Lawmaker

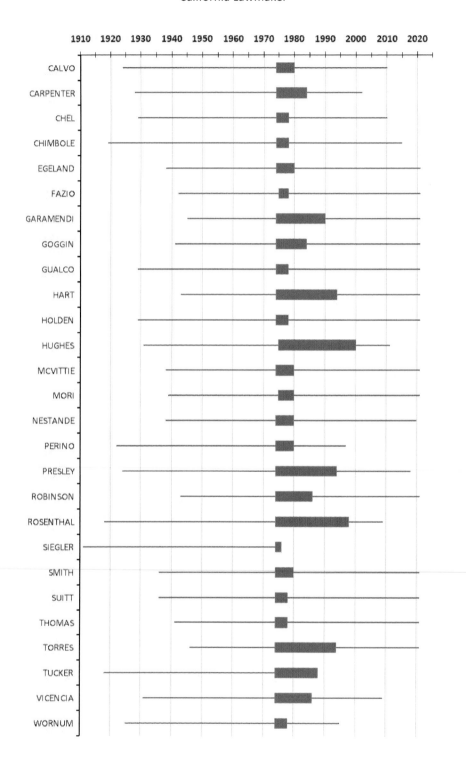

Class of 1974

The first class to use the modern session start date of the first Monday in December. Prior to 1975, the last time a legislative session started in a month other than January was 1877. This class included one state constitutional officer, Lt. Governor (and Insurance Commissioner) John Garamendi and three members of Congress; Garamendi, Bill Thomas, and Vic Fazio.

Assemblyman Alfred C. Siegler died during his first term at age 64. Curtis R. Tucker died in his seventh at age 70. One interesting note about this class is that it appears to have had more members who were the parents of later legislators than any other. Tucker, Nate Holden, and Brian Nestande each had a son who would serve in the Assembly.

Teresa Hughes, the longest-serving female legislator in state history, arrived as a late addition to this class through a special election. She would serve just over 25 years before terming out of the Senate in 2000.

Art Torres, who got his start as the Legislative Director for the United Farm Workers (UFW) union, was elected to the Assembly as a member of this class. He was one of the Senators who voluntarily left office in 1994 ahead of term limits and served as Chair of the California Democratic Party from 1995 to 2009.

Larry Chimbole, a former mayor of Palmdale, became the first Democrat in recent memory to represent the Antelope Valley in the Assembly[166]. Most legislators have ample friends and supporters while in office but few reach the point of being beloved by the community decades after leaving office. Chimbole was one of those rare legislators who remained widely respected and popular until his death more than two decades after leaving office.

---

[166] It wouldn't be until 2012 that another Democrat, Steve Fox, would represent that area in the lower house.

California Lawmaker

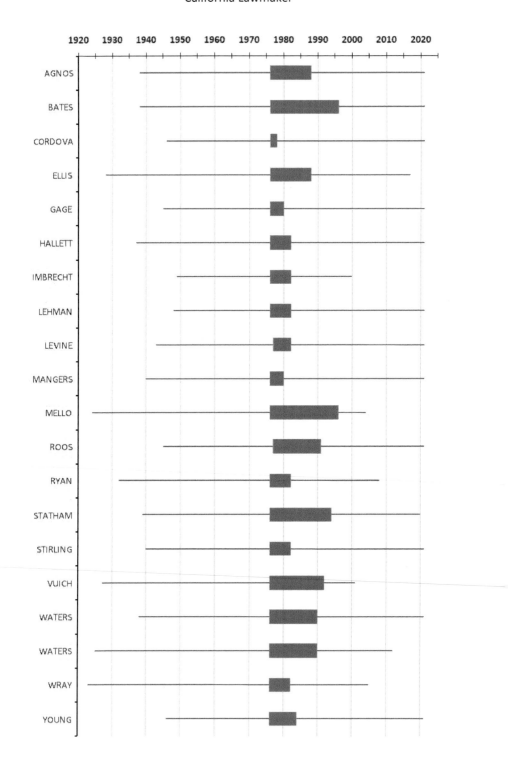

Class of 1976

Of the new members elected in 1976, the only one who started in the Senate was Rose Ann Vuich. Vuich was the first woman to serve in the Senate and was joined by Diane Watson in 1979. Their numbers grew and there were five female Senators by the time Vuich retired in 1992.

Another notable woman elected in 1976 was Carol Hallett, who became Assembly Minority Leader in her second term. This was the highest legislative position that a woman had achieved in the 60 years since they first became members. Since leaving the legislature in 1982, Hallett has had a diverse career, including service as an ambassador, Commissioner for the U.S. Customs Service, and Director of California's Department of Parks and Recreation.

Art Agnos had been a legislative staffer for nearly a decade before becoming a member himself. In 1973, while serving as a staffer for Assemblyman Leo McCarthy, Agnos was shot in the back twice during the Zebra Murders in San Francisco. By 1976, he was Chief of Staff to Speaker McCarthy and won had his first election by defeating Harvey Milk in the primary. He would serve in the Assembly until he was elected Mayor of San Francisco in 1988.

A good son of the State of Jefferson, Assemblyman Stan Statham is best remembered for his efforts in the early 1990s to promote the idea of dividing California into three states. After much investigation, Statham authored a bill[167] which would have placed an advisory question on the ballot in 1994 to gauge Californians willingness to split. The bill passed the Assembly easily, but wasn't able to gain traction in the Senate.

---

[167] Assembly Bill 3 (1993)

California Lawmaker

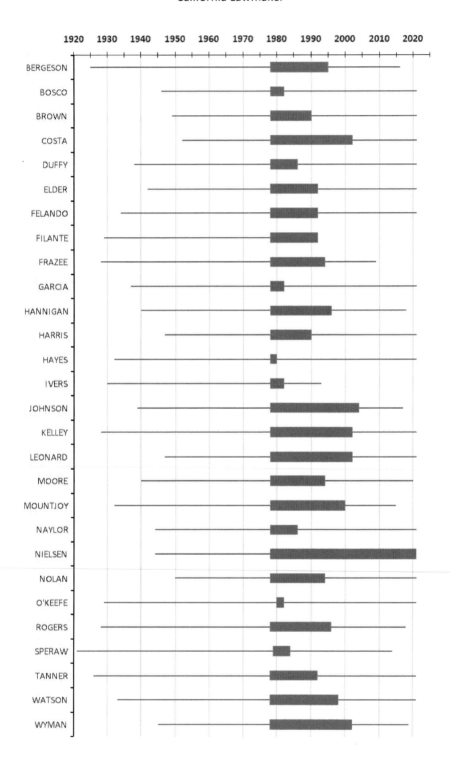

Class of 1978

The nineteen Republican members of the Class of 1978 were collectively called the "Prop 13 Babies" after the initiative that drove conservative voters to the polls in 1978. These Prop 13 babies included one state constitutional officer, Board of Equalization Member Bill Leonard. Leonard was one of four members of this class who would serve as Assembly Minority Leader (the others were Pat Nolan, Ross Johnson, and Bob Naylor). Johnson would also serve as Minority Leader in the Senate, as did classmate Jim Nielsen.

The class was also notable in that it included five new women to the legislature, the largest number up to that point. It also brought us the first two 1950s babies in the Legislature; Assemblymen Pat Nolan[168] (born 1950) and Jim Costa (born 1952). Costa would end up being the 1950s baby who served the longest in the legislature; 24 years between the two houses. Costa was one of three members of this class to be elected to Congress, the others were Diane Watson[169] and Douglas Bosco.

After three years as a lobbyist for the California Nurses Association, Jean M. Moorhead began her first term in 1978 as a Republican. In early 1981, she changed her registration to Democratic. Four years later, she changed her surname to Duffy after marrying former Assemblyman Gordon Duffy, whom she had served with during her first two terms[170].

Today, Nielsen is the last 1970s lawmaker still serving in the state legislature.

---

[168] Pat Nolan is the great-grandson of Pierre Agoura (for whom Agoura Hills is named).

[169] Diane Watson was only the second woman to serve in the State Senate. She later served as U.S. Ambassador to Micronesia.

[170] It wouldn't be until 2004 that a married couple (George and Sharon Runner) would serve together in the legislature.

California Lawmaker

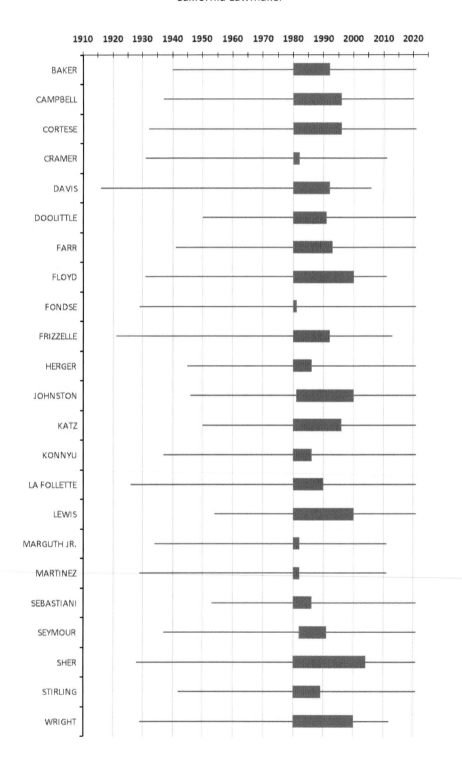

Class of 1980

One of the most notable (but unknown) legislators of the 1980s was Adrian Fondse. After a hard-fought campaign, Fondse was declared elected and sworn into the Assembly at the start of session in December 1980. The losing candidate, Patrick Johnston, requested a recount that lasted for most of December. By the time the legislature reconvened in January, the recount had found that Johnston had won by 35 votes.

On January 5th, the election was formally challenged and Johnston took Fondse's place[171]. John Seymour, elected to the Senate in a 1982 special election, would resign to accept an appointment to the U.S. Senate by Governor Pete Wilson in 1991. He remains the last California Republican to serve in the U.S. Senate.

Six members of this class would be elected to Congress, one of the highest numbers for any class[172]. Sam Farr, previously a Monterey County Supervisor, served in the Assembly from 1981 until his election to Congress in 1992[173]. As a second-generation legislator, Farr obviously felt a strong connection with his constituents and was a very visible part of life on the Central Coast for decades. He retired from Congress in 2017 after 35 years in elected office.

Byron Sher, a former Fulbright Scholar who served in the Assembly until 1996 and the Senate until 2004, focused much of his legislative energy on environmental issues. He authored the Groundwater Protection Act (1983), California Clean Air Act (1988), and the California Safe Drinking Water Act (1989).

---

[171] The 35 days that Fondse served were the shortest legislative career since Assemblyman Dana P. Eicke died in office 20 days into his first term in 1935.

[172] 177 members of the California Legislature have also served in Congress; 161 served in the House of Representatives, 14 served in the U.S. Senate, and two others (Assemblyman Charles N. Felton and State Senator Clair Engle) served in both houses.

[173] His father Fred Farr had served as a Senator from 1955 to 1966.

California Lawmaker

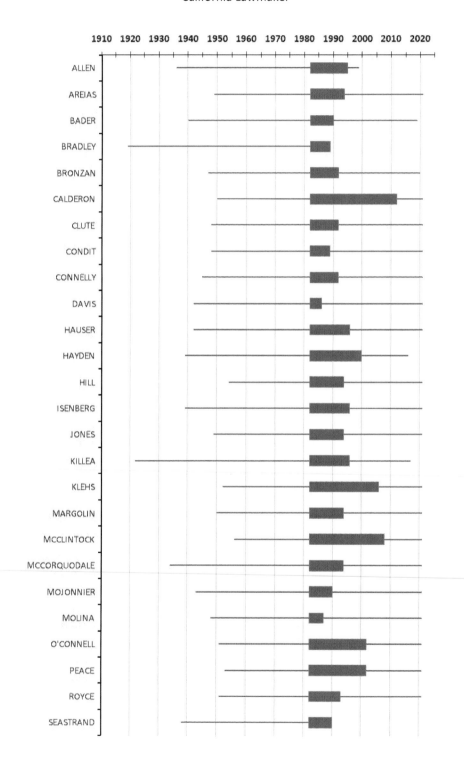

Class of 1982

The class of 1982 included four state constitutional officers; Governor Gray Davis, Secretary of State Bill Jones, Superintendent of Public Instruction Jack O'Connell and Board of Equalization Member Johan Klehs. It also included three Congressmen (Gary Condit, Tom McClintock, and Ed Royce). The final freshman legislator born in the 1910s was Bill Bradley (born 1919) who was a member of this class. Bradley was one of two members of this class to die in office; the other was Eric Seastrand in 1990. Doris Allen was elected to the Assembly in 1982 during her third attempt. In 1995 she would become the first female Assembly Speaker.

The two longest serving members of this class were Charles M. Calderon and McClintock, who each served 22 years. Calderon, who served as Majority Leader in both the Senate and Assembly, is the only person to hold both positions.

The class included some notable opposites. Lucy Killea was the first female legislator with war experience, having been a civilian intelligence analyst in the Army during World War II. She later served as a CIA analyst. Tom Hayden, who had founded Students for a Democratic Society and been married to Jane Fonda, was one of the most visible Vietnam War protesters.

Jack O'Connell unintentionally had the final word in a 145-year debate when he authored a bill that repealed various "obsolete laws" including the law against dueling. The law against dueling had been one of the more contentious points of debate during the 1849 Constitutional Convention, during which Delegate Louis Dent said;

"No clause that you can introduce in the Constitution will prevent a man from fighting a duel, if it be in defense of his honor. There are few men who will not risk their lives when their honor is at stake."[174]

---

[174] Report of the Debates in the Convention of California by John Ross Browne (J. T. Towers; 1850)

California Lawmaker

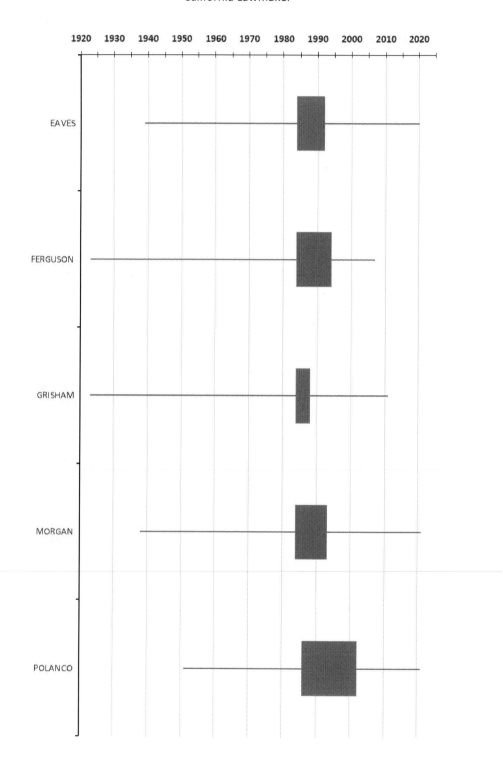

Class of 1984

The 1984 election brought only five new members to the legislature, making it the smallest freshman class ever. For comparison, the largest class of legislators had arrived just over a century before, with 102 new members[175]. One interesting thing about this class is the pairing of the birthdates; Grisham was three months older than Ferguson, while Morgan and Eaves were born five months apart.

Gil Ferguson was a U.S. Marine who fought in World War II, Korea, and Vietnam. Elected to the Assembly in 1984, he served 10 years. In 1986, he famously made a motion on the Assembly Floor to have Tom Hayden removed as a member for his support of the North Vietnamese during the war. After his death in 2007, Senator Tom McClintock noted;

> *"I have known many upstanding and exemplary leaders in the legislature during my 21 years here. The very finest of them passed away yesterday." – Senate Journal (May 7, 2007)*

Becky Morgan, the 32nd woman in the legislature, served almost 9 years in the Senate[176]. One of her most lasting legacies was authoring legislation to preserve and rehabilitate the Stanford Mansion as a place of historic interest.

Richard Polanco, who had previously been a staffer for Richard Alatorre and Governor Jerry Brown, arrived as an Assemblyman in a special election. He would found and chair the California Latino Legislative Caucus for ten years, and serve as Senate Majority Leader for five. The Latino Caucus' Polanco Fellowship is named for him.

---

[175] In 1880, the 80 members of the Assembly had a combined 26 years of prior legislative experience, while the Senate had 25 years.

[176] Morgan was the first California State Senator born in New Hampshire since Dr. Chester Rowell finished his final term in 1906. We have not had another since.

California Lawmaker

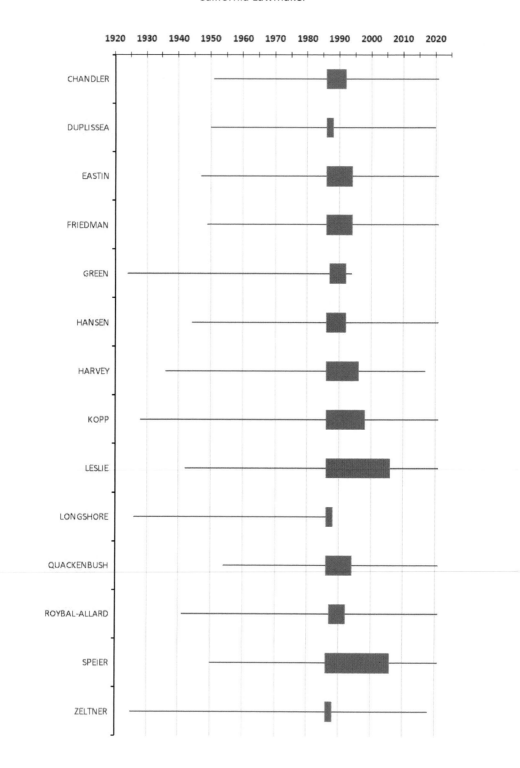

Class of 1986

This class included two state constitutional officers, Insurance Commissioner Chuck Quackenbush and Superintendent of Public Instruction Delaine Eastin, and two members of Congress; Jackie Speier and Lucille Roybal-Allard. The shortest-serving member of this class was Richard Longshore, a veteran of World War II, Korea, and Vietnam, who died in office during his first term. Quentin Kopp, a San Francisco County Supervisor, was unique because he was elected as an Independent, defeating both a Democrat (Lou Papan) and Republican (Russell Gray).

Tim Leslie, who had served as an Assembly committee consultant during the late 1960s, ran for Assembly in 1984 against former Republican Jean Duffy, losing narrowly. In 1986, Duffy declined another term and Leslie won easily. He would become the longest-serving legislator in the term limits era with partial terms (from special elections) giving him 9.5 years in the Senate and 6.5 years in the Assembly[177].

Jackie Speier, as a 28 year old Congressional staffer, was shot in the attack that killed Congressman Leo Ryan. After serving on the San Mateo County Board of Supervisors, she was elected to the Assembly where she authored the law establishing the California Family Code in 1992.

Bill Duplissea, who died in 2020, was one of a kind. Years after serving in the legislature, he became a lobbyist who poured his heart and his time into Capitol newcomers. A great storyteller, Bill would put his hand on your shoulder while talking about the old days to pull you a little bit closer when getting to a good part of the story. His death leaves a gap in the Capitol community and he will be deeply missed for years to come.

---

[177] Leslie also served later than most pre-term limits legislators. Of the 110 legislators elected before 1990, only four served later than his retirement in 2006; McClintock and Dymally until 2008, Charles Calderon until 2012 and Jim Nielsen.

California Lawmaker

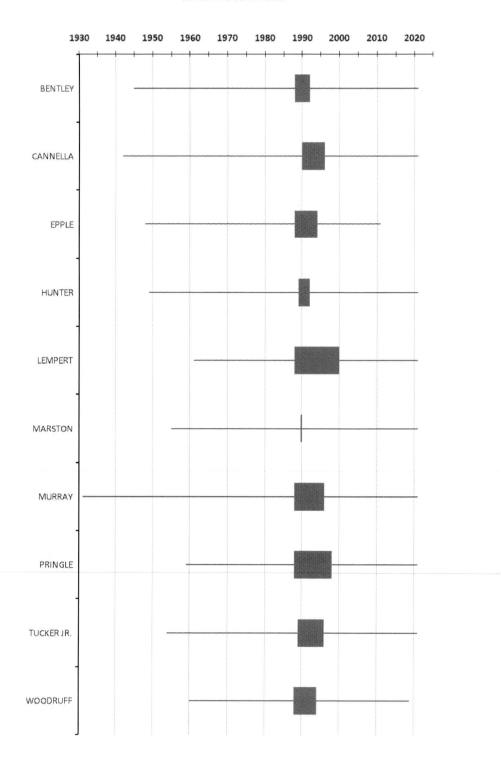

Class of 1988

Like the perfect wave roaring ashore at Steamer Lane, some moments seem like they were created to catapult people to greatness. 1989 was not one of those moments. The new legislators elected in 1988 landed in the legislature right before the start of term limits, facing short terms and a schedule that was poorly timed for moving to the Senate. Every single member of this class was an Assemblymember and not one made it to the Senate.

Of the ten members, five would leave due to term limits, one (Bentley) would decline a third term to run for Senate, and three (Hunter, Marston, and Woodruff) were defeated by members of the other party. The Class of 1989 also had the notable distinction of being the only one between 1970 and 2012 that didn't have a single member who later served in Congress.

Jeff Marston, elected in a 1990 special election, was defeated five months later when he ran for a full term[178]. In one of the great ironies, Marston (whose short tenure of 177 days limited him to a single chaptered bill) was the author of one of the most important initiatives in the past decade. As a co-chair of the California Independent Voter Project, Marston was a proponent of Proposition 14 (2010) which created California's Top Two Primary that has had a significant impact on the legislature in recent years.

The highest-ranking official in this class was Curt Pringle, who in one tumultuous year held the offices of Assembly Speaker, Majority Leader, and Minority Leader[179]. This class brought us our first legislators born in the 1960s; Assemblymen Paul Woodruff (born 1960) and Ted Lempert (born 1961).

---

[178] With just six months in office, Marston was shortest-serving member since Adrian Fondse in 1981, and the 8th-shortest serving legislator of the 20th century.

[179] Pringle is one of only two legislators to hold these three offices. It's ironic that the other is Willie L. Brown (who Pringle fought for the Speakership).

California Lawmaker

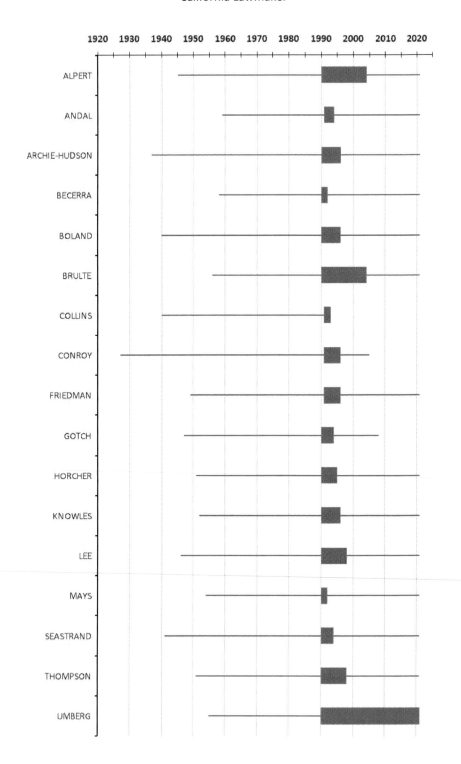

Class of 1990

Arriving in Sacramento a month after the passage of Proposition 140 (1990), the Class of 1990 included the first legislators subject to term limits from the moment they arrived. This class included B.T. Collins, a Special Forces Captain who had lost an arm and a leg in a grenade explosion in Vietnam. Collins, nicknamed "Captain Hook" for the steel hook that took the place of his right hand, was held in high regard by both parties, having held high-ranking positions in the administrations of both Jerry Brown and Pete Wilson. Within two years, would become the only member of this class to die in office.

The two youngest members of this class would go on to become constitutional officers. Xavier Becerra, elected at 32, served one term in the Assembly before being elected to Congress. He served there until 2017, when Governor Jerry Brown appointed him Attorney General[180].

Dean Andal, who arrived after winning a special election in 1991, was 31 when he assumed office. He left after three years to become a member of the State Board of Equalization. The third-youngest member of the class, Jim Brulte, became Minority Leader in his second year in the Assembly and organized the campaigns that would bring a Republican majority to the Assembly for the second time in recent memory. Brulte was the Republican nominee for Speaker during much of the Speakership battle of 1995[181].

Tom Umberg, a former Assistant U.S. Attorney, served two terms in the Assembly before leaving in 1994 to run for Attorney General. He lost, but became Deputy Director of the White House Office of National Drug Control Policy. Umberg returned to the Senate in 2018, which makes him the last-serving member of this class.

---

[180] Becerra was only the third former legislator to become Attorney General since 1900. The others were Bill Lockyer (1999-2007), George Deukmejian (1979-1983), and Robert Kenny (1943-1947).
[181] The most contentious Speakership battle ever was that of 1861, which took ten days and 109 rounds of voting to elect Ransom Burnell.

California Lawmaker

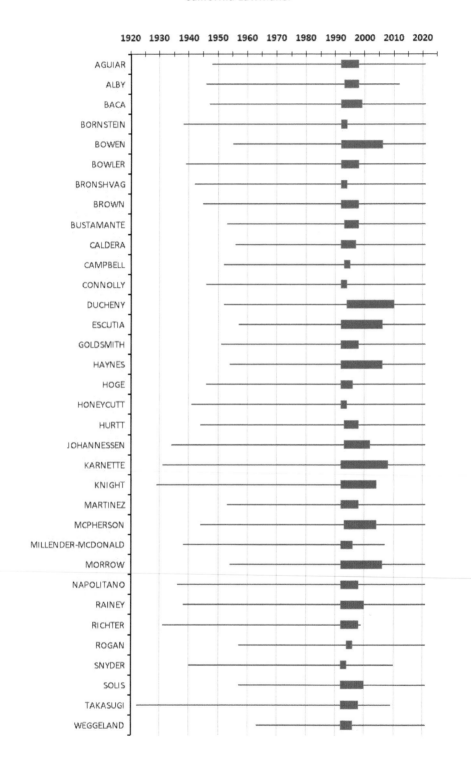

Class of 1992

This class included four state constitutional officers, Lt. Governor Cruz Bustamante, Secretaries of State Bruce McPherson and Debra Bowen, and Acting Board of Equalization Member Barbara Alby. Six members of this class served in Congress. Three of the women in this class went on to serve in Congress, the most of any legislative class.

Jim Rogan[182], the youngest of the special election arrivals during this session, spent just over a term in the Assembly before moving on to Congress. As a Congressman, Rogan served as one of the House Managers in the Impeachment Trial of President Clinton, a role that cost him his seat in 2000. Rogan wasn't alone in being a short-timer in the legislature; this class had more single-term Assemblymembers than any other since 1947.

The oldest member of this class was Nao Takasugi, who had been relocated to Arizona as part of the Japanese-American interment[183] during World War II. Takasugi, who was born in Oxnard in 1922, was interned at the Gila River camp in Arizona from 1942 to 1943, when he left to attend college in Philadelphia. His family returned to Oxnard after the war and he served as a member of the city council and as mayor before being elected to the Assembly.

Denise M. Ducheny, who arrived following an exceptionally close Assembly special election, became one of the great budget negotiators of the modern era, spending 11 years as a member of the budget conference committee. Ducheny's tireless work during 2009-10, during which the state struggled to solve a massive budget shortfall, was a contribution matched by few recent legislators.

---

[182] Rogan's book Rough Edges: My Unlikely Road from Welfare to Washington (WND Books; 2004) is a strikingly honest autobiography and one of the best books written by a legislator.

[183] The other California state legislators who were detained in internment camps were Paul T. Bannai (1973), Mike Honda (1996), George Nakano (1998), and Alan Nakanishi (2002).

California Lawmaker

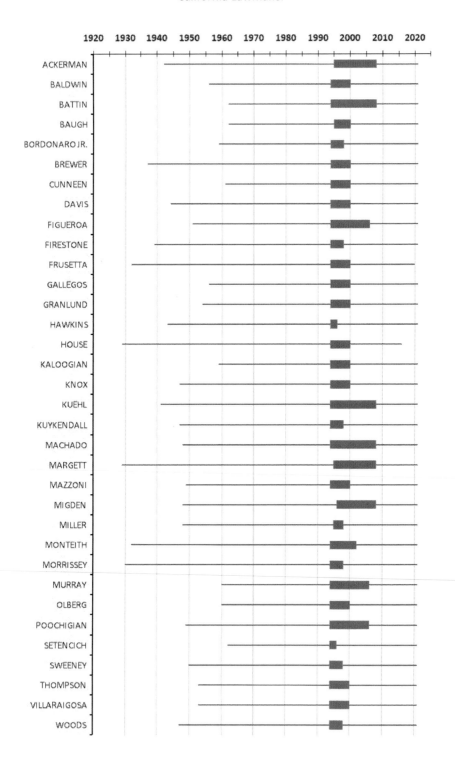

Class of 1994

Probably the most notable characteristic of this group was the partisan composition; Republicans made up two thirds of the class. This group would bring a Republican majority in the Assembly for the first time since 1970 and be a part of one of the most memorable sessions in modern history.

In addition to Senate pro Tem Don Perata, this was one of only two classes since the 1930s that included two Assembly Speakers; Brian Setencich and Antonio Villaraigosa[184]. Setencich, elected Speaker after just ten months as a legislator, had a Speakership for the record books. He had the shortest tenure as Speaker since F. C. Clowdsley in 1934 and the shortest tenure in the Assembly (two years) of any Speaker since Hugh M. La Rue in 1883. Setencich was also notable as the first and only Assembly Speaker from Fresno County[185].

Antonio Villaraigosa, the second Speaker of this class, served from 1998 to 2000. He served as Mayor of Los Angeles from 2005 to 2013. Villaraigosa ran for Governor in 2018 but finished third in the primary behind Gavin Newsom and Republican John Cox. Carole Migden served as a member of the Board of Equalization from 2003 to 2004.

Since the introduction of the recall in 1913, only five California state legislators have been successfully recalled. The year with the most recalls was 1995, which saw the recalls of Paul Horcher and Doris Allen and the resulting arrival of Assemblymembers Scott Baugh and Gary G. Miller. Baugh served five years in the Assembly before leaving in 2000.

---

[184] By comparison, the last class to include two Senate President pro Tems was 1933 with Senators Ben Hulse and Harold J. Powers.
[185] Cruz Bustamante, who became Speaker eleven months after Setencich lost the position, represented Fresno and Tulare, but was from Tulare County.

California Lawmaker

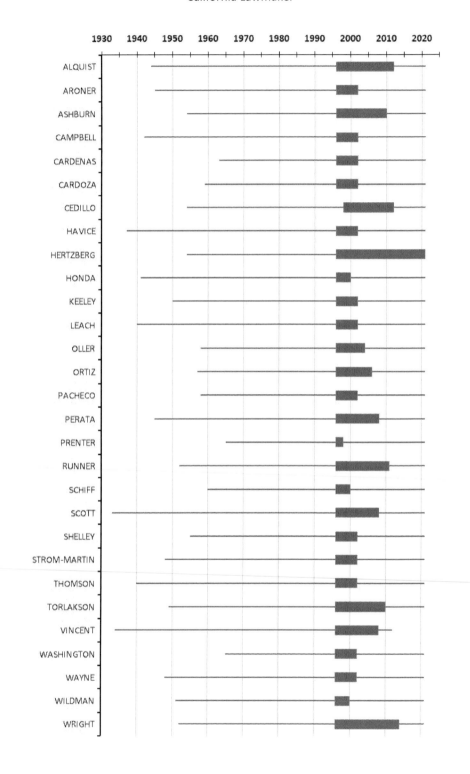

Class of 1996

This class included three state constitutional officers, Secretary of State Kevin Shelley, Superintendent of Public Instruction Tom Torlakson, and Board of Equalization Member George Runner as well as four Members of Congress (Cardoza, Cardenas, Honda, and Schiff).

The Class of 1997 included a lower-house royal flush; an Assembly Speaker (Hertzberg), Speaker pro Tem (Keeley), Majority Leader (Shelley), and Minority Leader (Pacheco) as well a Senate President pro Tem (Perata). In 2014 Hertzberg became the first Assembly Speaker in more than 80 years to be elected to the Senate.

Gil Cedillo, elected following the resignation of Assemblyman Louis Caldera, was the only member of this class to arrive through a special election[186]. The timing of his special election allowed Cedillo to serve nearly seven in the Assembly, making him the longest-serving Assemblyman under California's first terms law.

During his time in office, Cedillo dedicated his efforts to expanding services for undocumented workers in California. In his final term, he authored the California DREAM Act, which permits college students without legal immigration status to compete for scholarships and legally attend California public colleges and universities.

Floor speeches in favor or opposition to legislation very rarely sway votes. One notable exception was Rod Wright, a gifted speaker who could hold the undivided attention of the house. Although he usually voted with his party, Wright occasionally sided with Republicans on critical votes, much to the frustration of Senate leadership.

Wright was indicted in 2010 on charges that he had lied about his residency while filing to run for Senate in 2008 and was placed on an involuntary suspension from the Senate during the trial in 2014. Wright resigned from the Senate after being convicted, and spent just over an hour in jail. He was pardoned by Governor Jerry Brown in 2018.

---

[186] Louis Caldera had resigned to become the Secretary of the Army (1998-2001).

California Lawmaker

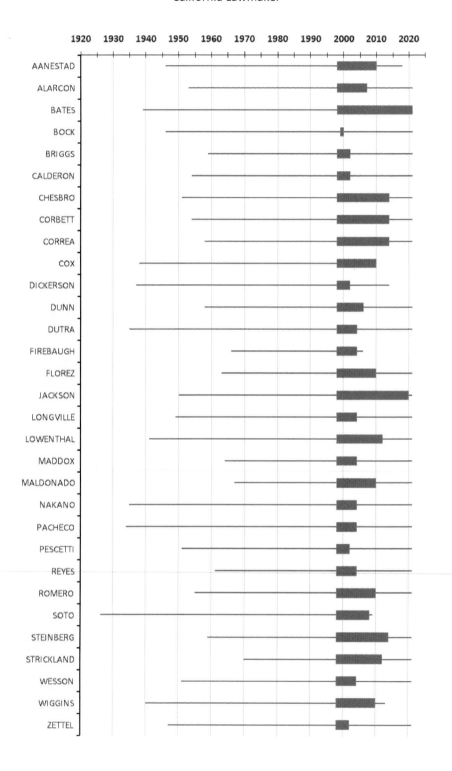

Class of 1998

The Class of 1998 was an interesting one that transitioned the legislature fully into the term limits era. The last of the pre-term Limits Senators had finally termed out. It was also a transition year in another way; this class included both the final 1920s baby to arrive in the legislature (Nell Soto, born 1926) as well as the first legislator born in the 1970s; Tony Strickland (born 1970).

This class included one state constitutional officer, Lieutenant Governor Abel Maldonado. It also included a large number of legislative leaders, including Speaker Herb Wesson, Senate President pro Tem Darrell Steinberg, a decade worth of Senate Majority Leaders[187], Senate Minority Leader Patricia Bates, as well as Assembly Majority Leader Marco A. Firebaugh (the youngest Democrat of the class).

It also included Audie Bock, the first non-major party candidate elected to a first term in California since 1916. As a member of the Green Party, Bock won a special election against six-term Assemblyman Elihu Harris by 327 votes.

One of the youngest members of the class, Ken Maddox, had the interesting footnote of being the first leapling[188] to serve in the California Legislature in more than 40 years.

Senator Dave Cox, one of the older members, was the only one to die in office. Two others, Nell Soto and Marco A. Firebaugh, died just months after leaving office.

---

[187] Senate Majority Leaders Gloria Romero (2004-2009), Dean Florez (2009-2010) and Ellen Corbett (2010-2014) were all members of this class.

[188] "Leaplings" are people born on February 29th (Leap Day). The other four known Leaplings who have served in the California Legislature were William Tell Coleman and Governor Washington Bartlett (born 1824), Fred C. Gerdes (born 1880), and Gordon A. Fleury (born 1916).

California Lawmaker

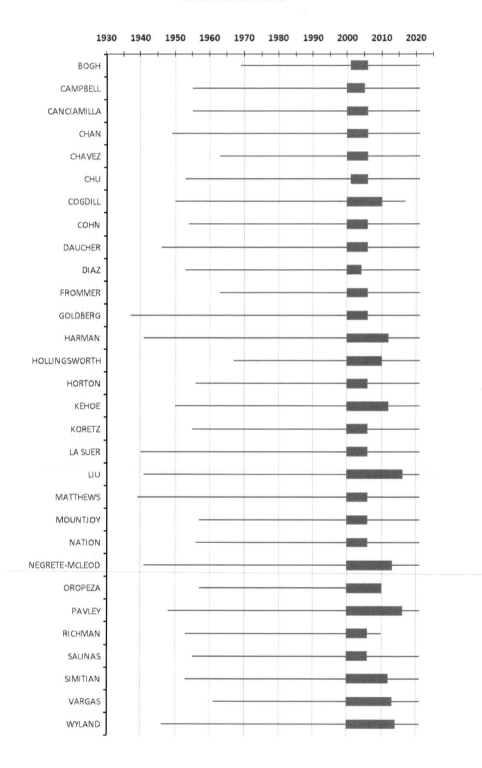

Class of 2000

This class was an outlier in that seven of the ten oldest members of this class were women, something that had not been seen before. The class included two state constitutional officers, Board of Equalization Members Judy Chu and Jerome Horton. During their final terms in the Assembly, both Chu and Horton ran against each other in a hotly contested race for the Board of Equalization; Chu won.

A little more than two years into the four-year term, Chu won a Congressional seat in a special election. Governor Schwarzenegger appointed Horton to fill the vacancy, which was confirmed by the legislature with only a single no vote[189].

The youngest member of the class at the start of the session was Dennis Hollingsworth[190], who served only a single Assembly term before being elected to the Senate. In his final Senate term, Hollingsworth agreed to author a bill proposed by three junior staffers who felt strongly that it was unfair to include nearly all (but not all) statewide officials on the Governor's line of succession[191].

The oldest member of the class was Jackie Goldberg, an active member of the Berkeley Free Speech Movement in the mid-1960s, who today is an active member of the Los Angeles Unified School District Board. The youngest woman in this class, Jenny Oropeza, died in office as a State Senator in 2010.

The most significant legislation authored by a member of this class was AB 32 (2006) by Assemblywoman Fran Pavley. AB 32, "The Global Warming Solutions Act of 2006," required California to reduce global warming emissions back to 1990 levels by 2020, a reduction of 25%.

---

[189] That no vote came from Assemblyman Mike Eng, husband of Judy Chu.

[190] Russ Bogh, elected in an early-session special election, was two and a half years younger.

[191] SB 1530 (2008), drafted by Chris Nguyen, added the Superintendent of Public Instruction, Insurance Commissioner, and Chair of the Board of Equalization to the line of gubernatorial succession.

California Lawmaker

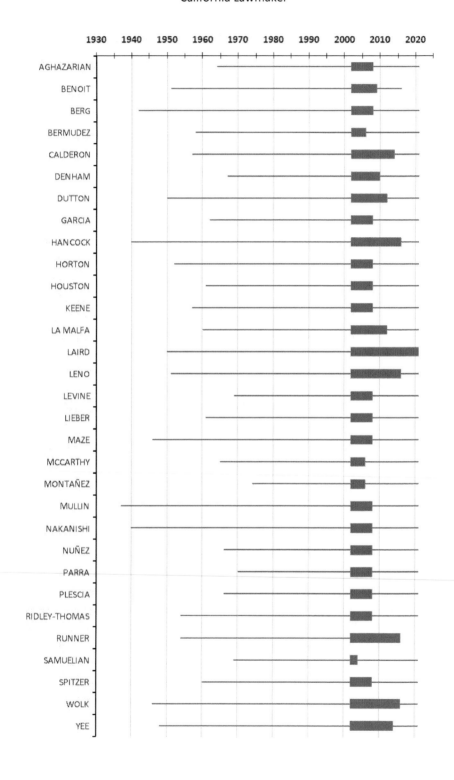

Class of 2002

One notable member of this class was Cindy Montanez, the youngest woman to ever serve in the legislature. Another was Mark Leno, who would serve as Budget Chair in both houses and help guide the state through some of the most challenging budget problems since the Great Depression.

Three Republican members of this class became Members of Congress; Kevin McCarthy (in 2006), Jeff Denham (in 2010), and Doug La Malfa (in 2012)[192].

Gene Mullin and his classmate Mark Ridley-Thomas each had a son who arrived as a member of the Class of 2013.

This class also included Leland Yee and Ronald S. Calderon, whose later years in the Senate were stained by criminal convictions and incarceration in federal prisons. Calderon's office at the State Capitol was raided by FBI agents on an evening in June 2013, and in early 2014 he was indicted on 24 corruption charges. He pleaded guilty to several charges in 2016 and was sentenced to 42 months in federal prison.

The arrest of Senator Yee remains one of the most shocking events in the recent history. Prior to the legislature, Yee had been a child psychologist and his concerns about the damage that violent video games could cause in young minds led him to author a bill on the subject that was so restrictive that it was overturned by the U.S. Supreme Court[193].

It's hard to explain the shock the Capitol community felt when he was indicted on arms trafficking charges. After more than four years in prison, Yee was released in June 2020.

---

[192] Congressmen Denham and La Malfa also shared a fantastic university as their alma mater; Cal Poly San Luis Obispo.

[193] In June 2011, the U.S. Supreme Court ruled that Yee's Assembly Bill 1179 (2005) violated the First Amendment. (Brown v. Entertainment Merchants Association, 08-1448)

California Lawmaker

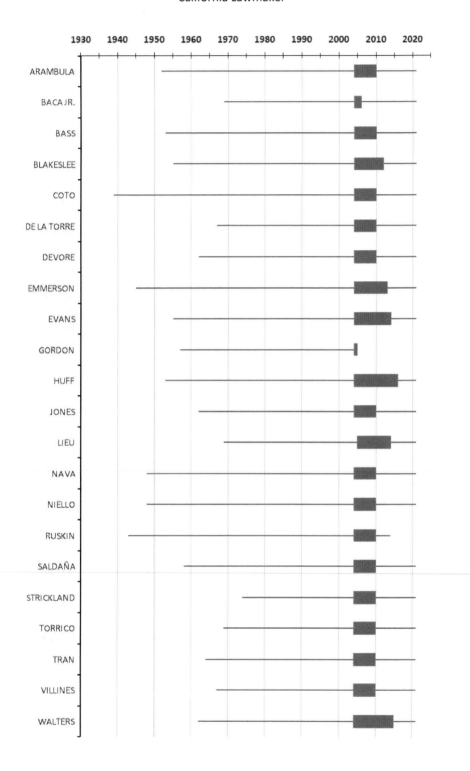

Class of 2004

This class had the very last freshman legislator born in the 1930s; Assemblyman Joe Coto (born 1939). It's also the most recent class that does not have a single member currently serving in the legislature. This class had one constitutional officer, Insurance Commissioner Dave Jones, and three members who were elected to Congress (Ted Lieu[194], Karen Bass, and Mimi Walters).

Bass was the highest-ranking member of the class (Assembly Speaker, 2008-2010) and the first former Assembly Speaker to become a member of Congress in 108 years[195]. The class also included Assembly Majority Leaders (Alberto Torrico and Lori Saldaña), a Senate Minority Leader (Bob Huff), and two Assembly Minority Leaders (Sam Blakeslee and Mike Villines).

One major negative result of term limits was that legislators frequently didn't master a policy area until shortly before they termed out. A sad example of this was Assemblyman Ira Ruskin. Long involved in local educational efforts, Ira Ruskin arrived in 2005 with a strong interest in education. He was a member of the Higher Education committee for six years and during his final term, Ruskin was made co-chair of a 20-member joint committee that conducted a deep review of the Master Plan for Higher Education.

The committee made a number of recommendations to improve the system but the final report was released too late to result in legislation before the end of Ruskin's final term. He was an early candidate for Senate in 2012, but was diagnosed with "incurable brain cancer and would retire from politics.[196]" Ira Ruskin died in 2014.

---

[194] Ted Lieu is the only member of the California Legislature to be elected to <u>both</u> the Assembly and Senate in special elections.

[195] Before Bass, the most recent former Speaker to become a Member of Congress was Frank L. Coombs (Speaker in 1891 and 1897, Congressman in 1901-1903). Speaker Sam L. Collins was a Member of Congress in 1933-1937 before being elected Speaker in 1947-1952.

[196] Source is an emailed press release by Ruskin dated May 13, 2011.

California Lawmaker

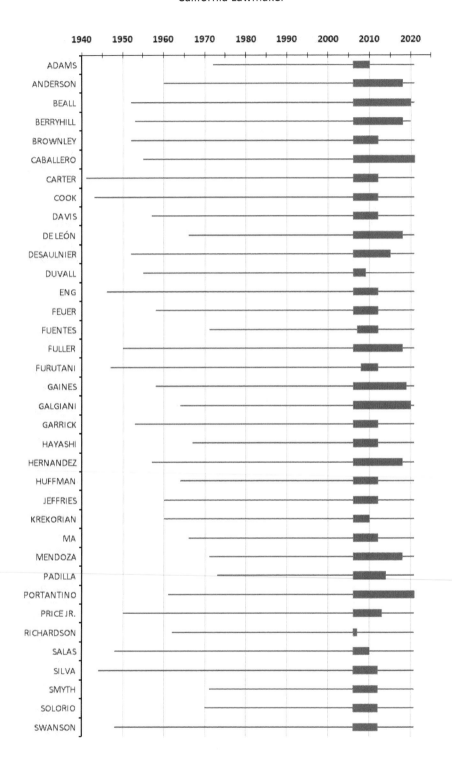

Class of 2006

This class included three state constitutional officers, Secretary of State Alex Padilla, State Treasurer Fiona Ma, and Board of Equalization member Ted Gaines as well as five members elected to Congress (Julia Brownley, Paul Cook, Mark DeSaulnier, Jared Huffman, and Laura Richardson). In 2021, Padilla was appointed to the U.S. Senate by Governor Newsom, becoming California's first state lawmaker to serve in the U.S. Senate since John Seymour in 1991-1992.

Laura Richardson was the first member of the class to depart the legislature, being elected to Congress just nine months into the new term. During her 261 days in the State Assembly, Richardson authored 20 bills and one resolution, of which five bills and one resolution were chaptered into law.

The class also included Senate President pro Tem Kevin De León, who led the Senate for nearly four years and ran a spirited campaign for U.S. Senate in 2018 and Senate Minority Leader Jean Fuller, the first woman to hold that post.

Anna Caballero, who left after her second Assembly term to run an ill-fated campaign for state Senate, returned to the Capitol for a final Assembly term in 2016. Because of her absence, Caballero had the distinction of being the last Assemblymember forced from office by the original term limits law. Today Caballero is a member of the State Senate, having won a second campaign for that office in 2018.

The class also included Tom Berryhill, the son of former Senator Clare L. Berryhill (class of 1969) and brother of Bill, who was elected to the Assembly the following session. Starting in 2008, the Berryhills were the first brothers to serve together in the same house since John and Robert McCarthy served in the Senate together in 1955-1958. Unlike the Berryhills, who were both Republicans, the Senators McCarthy were from different parties (John was a Republican and Robert was a Democrat).

California Lawmaker

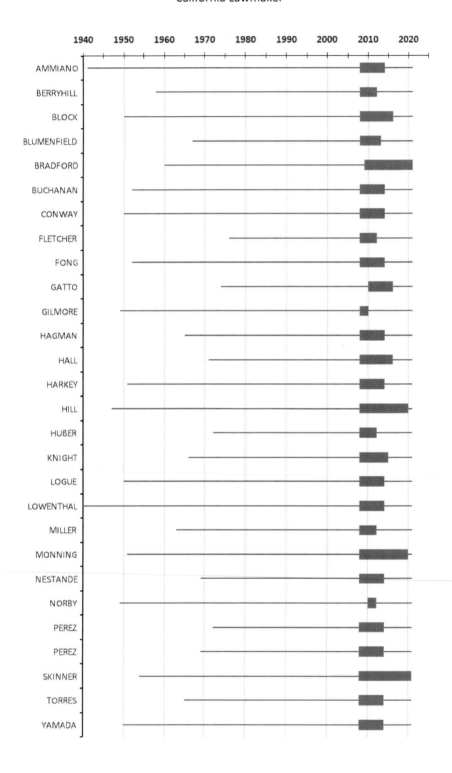

Class of 2008

Three members of this class were children of former legislators (Berryhill, Knight, and Nestande). The class would produce one constitutional officer, Board of Equalization Member Diane L. Harkey, and five legislative leaders; Assembly Speaker John A. Perez, Senate Majority Leader Bill Monning, Assembly Majority Leader V. Manuel Perez, and Assembly Minority Leader Connie Conway. Another two members, Steve Knight and Norma J. Torres, were elected to Congress.

This class was unique in that it was the last to be composed of only Assemblymembers, and nearly two decades into term limits, most Assembly seats had turned over five or six times since 1990. Knowing that their time in the legislature would be short, nearly half the left the Assembly before terming out.

One member who voluntarily left the legislature early was Danny Gilmore. As a Republican who had been narrowly elected from a previously Democratic district, his arrival in Sacramento was seen a thorn in the side of the house leadership. Gilmore faced delays to hiring his staff and opening offices and his legislation (much of which was inspired by his 30 years as a Highway Patrol officer) had trouble getting out of the Assembly. After two years, Gilmore declined to seek a second term, saying that "frustration" was the central theme of his tenure.

Elected more than half-way through the session, Mike Gatto was eligible to serve another three Assembly terms. These extra five months made him the senior Assemblymember during the 2015-16 Session as well as the final individual to serve as Dean of the Assembly.

In his role as Dean during the least experienced session in generations, Gatto frequently tweeted advice and warnings to his colleagues. One example; "The worst kind of manipulators are those who create delays, and then invoke the late hour to urge an unwise move."[197]

---

[197] Tweet by Assemblyman Mike Gatto (@mikegatto) 4/15/2016
https://twitter.com/mikegatto/status/721079706393534464

California Lawmaker

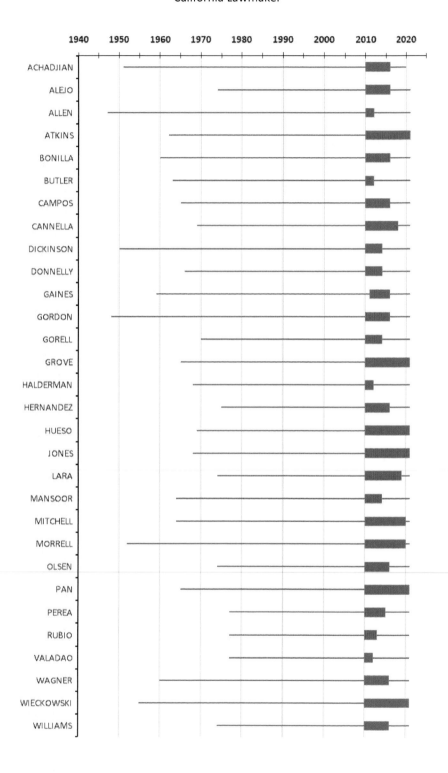

Class of 2010

A class filled with a number of impressive legislators, this class will likely be remembered as the one that brought Toni G. Atkins to Sacramento. Atkins, a former staffer and city councilmember, was elevated to Assembly Majority Leader in her first term, which she leveraged to become Assembly Speaker at the end of her second. Elected to the State Senate in 2016, she became President pro Tem in 2018, the first person to have led both houses of the legislature since the unusually named Ransom Burnell in 1864.

The class also included a constitutional officer, Insurance Commissioner Ricardo Lara, as well three legislative leaders; Assembly Speaker pro Tem Nora Campos, Senate Minority Leader Shannon Grove, and Assembly Minority Leader Kristin Olsen. According to my research, Shannon Grove was the first female Californian state legislator to have served in the military[198].

The legislative powerhouse of this class was Luis Alejo, who arrived in Sacramento with what appeared to be a full calendar for what he hoped to accomplish in his next six years. Alejo combined a strong coalition-building strategy with a sense of what he hoped to accomplish and dominated his second term, authoring two of the three most significant bills of the session[199].

Assemblymembers Betsy Butler and Michael Allen were defeated by fellow Democrats when they ran for second terms. Linda Halderman, echoing Danny Gilmore the session before, declined to run for a second term, saying of Sacramento "I never thought I would be in a profession bloodier than trauma surgery."[200]

---

[198] Lucy Killea (first elected in 1982) had been a civilian Army employee.

[199] Alejo's AB 10 (2013) raised the minimum wage to $10/hour by 2012 and AB 60 (2013) required the DMV to issue driver licenses to applicants unable to prove legal immigration status.

[200] "Lawmakers are tense, tired and goofy in the waning hours of the legislative session" by Shane Goldmacher, Los Angeles Times; 10 September 2012.

California Lawmaker

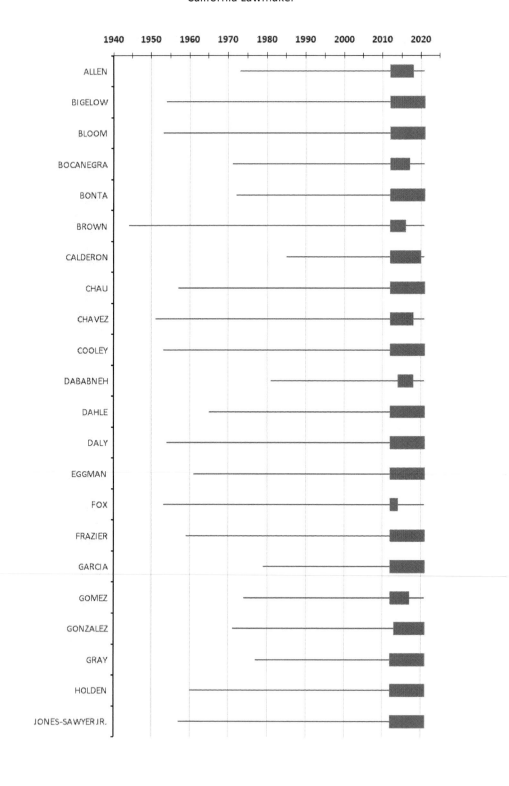

Class of 2012

The Class of 2013 was a massive one; 39 new members on the first day of session[201], which grew to 44 by the end of the session. This was the largest group of new legislators in a single session since the 1930s and (because a 2012 ballot proposition) the first term limits era class to be eligible to serve longer than a decade in a single house. The first member of this class to become a constitutional officer was Shirley Weber, who was appointed Secretary of State in January 2021.

The Class of 2012 brought the first legislator born in the 1980s; Assemblyman Ian C. Calderon (born 1985). Elected in a hard fought campaign[202], Calderon was the youngest member of the Assembly in 2013 at age 27, a title he lost before the end of the session when Sebastian Ridley-Thomas (age 26) was elected that December.

On March 10, 2016, Calderon became the youngest Assembly Majority Leader in state history (at age 30), displacing Walter J. Karabian (class of 1967) who became Majority Leader at age 33. In addition to Calderon and Ridley-Thomas (both sons of former State Senators), this class included three other sons of former legislators; Assemblymen Chris Holden, Kevin Mullin, and Sebastian Ridley-Thomas.

Since 2014, Kevin Mullin has served as Speaker pro Tem, a role in which most legislators only last a session or two. It's one of the most challenging positions in the legislature, requiring deep familiarity with parliamentary procedure, and attention to detail. It's like directing a stage production and also playing a central role, while additionally trying to keep track of 79 other actors who may be urgently trying to get your attention.

In 2021, Mullin begins his seventh year in the role, making him the longest Speaker pro Tem since Carlos Bee in 1974.

---

[201] The Class of 1967 had 41 new members on the first day of session but no special elections.
[202] Calderon narrowly won a spot in the 2012 General election when he defeated Rudy Bermudez by 337 votes.

California Lawmaker

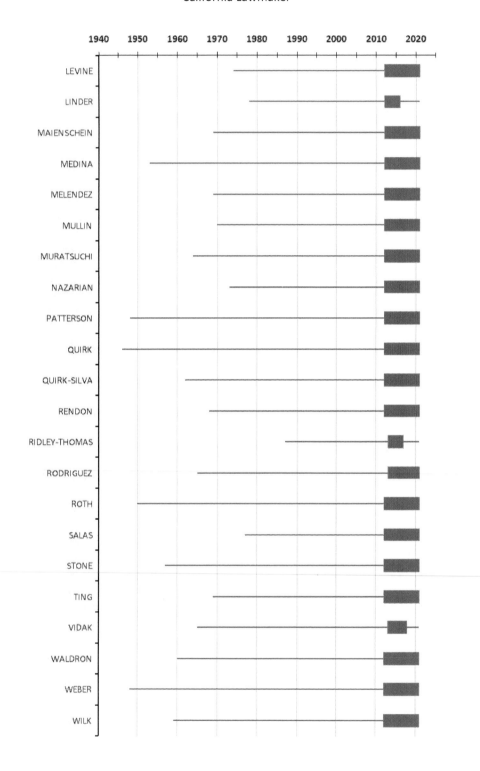

Another notable member of the Class of 2012 is Assembly Speaker Anthony Rendon, the first legislator under term limits 2.0 to hold that office. Rendon, a thoughtful and friendly legislator, is notable for the approach he brought to the office. In contrast to several Speakers in the years since Willie Brown, whose leadership style was described as the "Imperial Speakership," Rendon has regularly reached out to his colleagues, treating them as a second constituency.

Other members of this class include Assembly Minority Leaders Brian Dahle and Marie Waldron, as well as Congressman Jimmy Gomez. Dahle was elected to the Senate in 2019 and his wife Megan won his vacant Assembly seat in the resulting special election.

Major General Richard Roth brought a unique perspective that the Legislature hadn't seen in more than a century. According to current research[203], Roth is one of at least five Generals to serve in the Senate. The others were General Mariano G. Vallejo of the Mexican Army, Brigadier General Thomas J. Green of the Texian Volunteer Army, Civil War era generals Brigadier General George S. Evans of the Union Army, and Brigadier General Edward McGarry of the United States Volunteers.

After a close reelection in 2018[204], Assemblyman Brian Maienschein announced in early 2019 that he had changed his party affiliation from Republican to Democratic. Although not unprecedented, mid-term changes are exceedingly rare. In fact, it has only happened fourteen times in state history.

Previously, the last time a Republican became a Democrat mid-term was Senator Milton Marks in January 1986. The last mid-term change from Democrat to Republican was Senator Jack B. Tenney in 1944.

Eleven months later, Assemblyman Chad Mayes changed his party affiliation from Republican to No Party Preference.

---

[203] Research into early legislators is ongoing and there is still a lot to learn.
[204] According to the final count, Maienschein defeated Democratic challenger Sunday Gover by 607 out of nearly 200,000 cast in the contest.

California Lawmaker

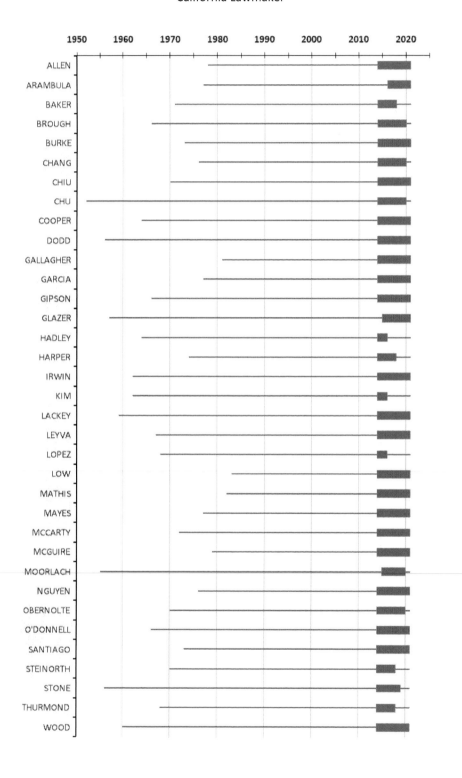

Class of 2014

Although not as large as the class before it, this class had a unique feel. Reflecting California's historic role as a melting pot, it included a higher than average number of foreign-born members; Ling Ling Chang and Kansen Chu from Taiwan, Young Kim from South Korea, Janet Nguyen from the former South Vietnam, Patty Lopez from Mexico, and John M. W. Moorlach from Netherlands.

As of early 2020, the members of the Class of 2014 included one constitutional officer, Superintendent of Public Instruction Tony Thurmond, one member of legislative leadership (Assembly Minority Leader Chad Mayes), and two members of Congress; Young Kim and Jay Obernolte.

This second batch of new term limits legislators was more adventurous than the first. Six months into her term, Ling Ling Chang announced that she would be leaving the Assembly at the end of her first term to run for the Senate. Chang lost the election in 2016, but was elected to the Senate in a 2018 recall of Senator Josh Newman.

David Hadley, Young Kim, and Tom Lackey each arrived by beating a member of the other party, while the biggest surprise came from Patty Lopez who ran a lightly funded campaign that defeated first-termer Raul Bocanegra. Hadley, Kim, and Lopez would each be defeated while seeking reelection after their single term.

The last member of this class to be elected was Senator Vanessa Delgado, who served for just 110 days after winning a special election[205]. The sliver of term remaining for her to serve was so small that there was some speculation that she might decline to assume office[206]. Instead, Delgado took the oath of office and immediately jumped into the hectic rush of the end of session. In her brief time, she managed to get two bills passed by the legislature, including one which was signed into law.

---

[205] Delgado's tenure was the briefest ever by a female legislator.

[206] The last person elected to the State Senate who declined to assume office was Samuel Brannan in 1853.

California Lawmaker

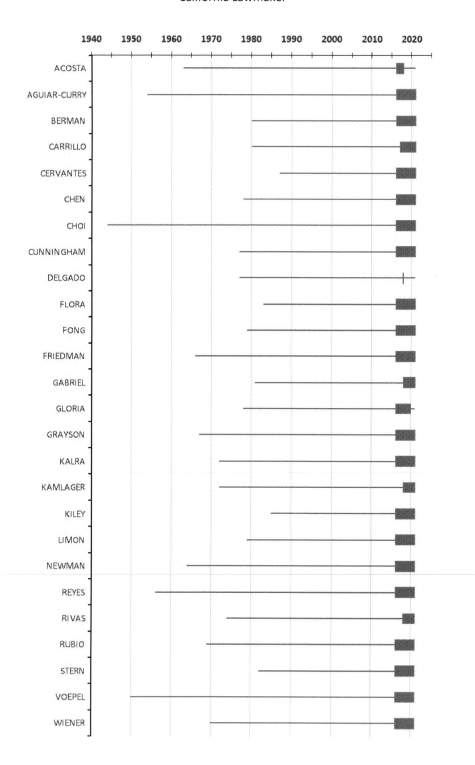

Class of 2016

The twenty-six members of the Class of 2016 included eighteen Democrats and eight Republicans. Dr. Steven S. Choi, born in 1944, arrived as the oldest freshman Assemblyman since the end of World War II. At the other end of the spectrum, Sabrina Cervantes was the new youngest member of the legislature (she was born two months after Sebastian Ridley-Thomas). Like the class before, the members of this class include some international arrivals; Ash Kalra was born in Canada, Blanca Rubio in Mexico, and Choi in South Korea.

This class also saw the arrival of Senator Josh Newman, who narrowly defeated Assemblywoman Ling Ling Chang in their contest for Senate District 29. After being recalled in mid-2018, Newman spent the rest of the term preparing for what would have been his first reelection. In 2020, Chang and Newman faced each other for a third time, with Newman winning (and becoming the state's first legislator reelected after being recalled).

Kevin Kiley used his experience as a prosecutor to become one of the most outspoken legislators in challenging the large number of executive orders issued by Governor Newsom during the COVID pandemic. Kiley won reelection in 2020 with more votes than any other Assembly Republican in state history. Another Republican with trial experience, former Deputy District Attorney Jordan Cunningham (and former Senate Fellow)[207], has brought a more collegial attitude.

Assemblyman Randy Voepel, who served in the Navy, was the legislature's first Vietnam veteran since Paul Cook termed out in 2012 (and likely the last).

---

[207] As of January 2021, the legislature has one former Senate Fellows (Cunningham) and two former Assembly Fellows (James Gallagher and Patrick O'Donnell).

California Lawmaker

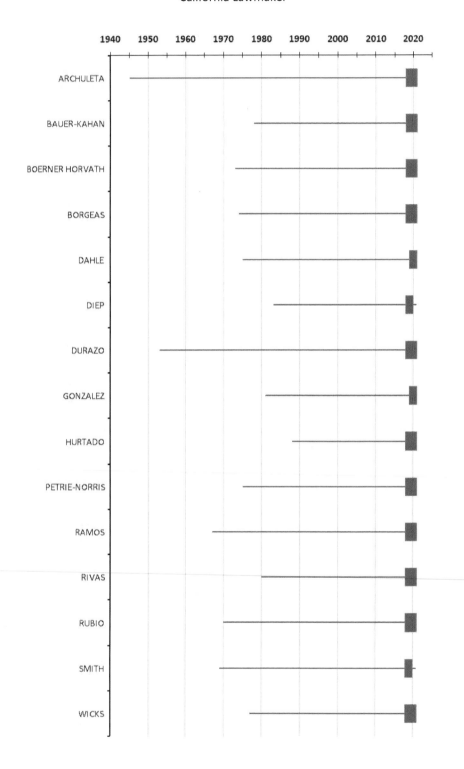

Class of 2018

After nearly 170 years of a long and difficult relationship between California's native population and state government, Assemblyman James C. Ramos became the first state legislator born on tribal land (he was born on the San Manuel Indian Reservation). Just months after Ramos was elected, Governor Gavin Newsom issued a formal apology to the tribes of California for their historic treatment by the state[208].

In the Central Valley, Melissa Hurtado defeated incumbent Senator Andy Vidak to become California's youngest-ever female Senator. At the other end of the spectrum was her Senate colleague Bob Archuleta, who was the oldest freshman legislator since Assemblyman Albert I. Stewart (age 74) was inaugurated in January 1945.

At just over 63,000 residents, San Benito County is a fairly small county that has for generations been packed into districts dominated by more populous coastal or valley neighbors. Elected in 2018, Assemblyman Robert Rivas became the first legislator from San Benito County since Peter Frusetta termed out in 2000. He was also the first San Benito County Supervisor to be elected to the legislature since State Senator Thomas Flint Jr. in 1900.

Farther south in Los Angeles, Susan Rubio was elected to the Senate, making her and her sister Assemblywoman Blanca Rubio the first pair of sisters to serve in the legislature.

Running for her second term in 2020, Buffy Wicks received more votes than any other Assembly candidate in state history, while Tyler Diep, who started the session as the sole Assembly Republican freshman[209], was defeated in the primary.

---

[208] Executive Order N-15-19 was issued June 18, 2019

[209] Until the election of Megan Dahle in November 2019, this was the first class with a single freshman Assembly Republican since Assemblyman Milton Marks (of San Francisco) was elected in 1958.

California Lawmaker

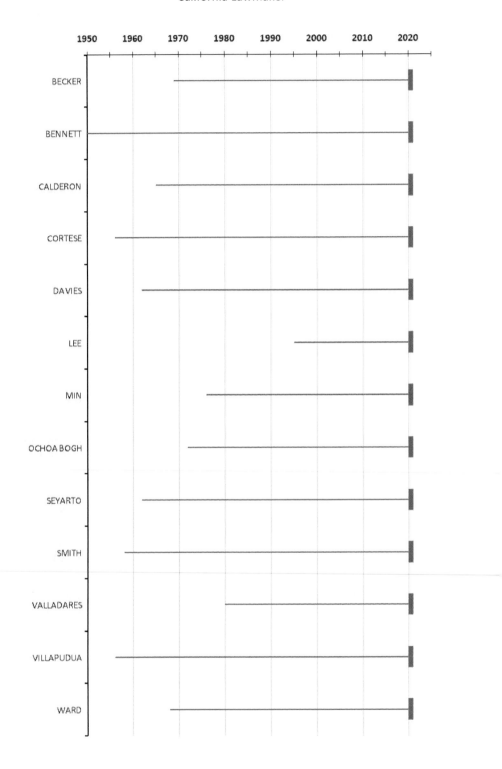

Class of 2020

The 2020 election was the first presidential election in a generation that saw the Assembly Republican caucus grow[210]. The Republicans ended the 2019-2020 session with seventeen members and a vacancy after losing two members to party changes early in the session. Suzette Martinez Valladares' victory in an Assembly seat that had been flipped just the session before was a rare and historic victory for the Republicans. The Republicans' luck didn't extend to the Senate, where David Min and Josh Newman (Class of 2016) won two previously Republican seats in the Senate, bringing Democrats to their highest percentage in the upper house since 1883.

Nearly a quarter of the new class has a relative who has served in the legislature; Senator David Cortese is the son of Assemblyman Dom Cortese (class of 1980), Senator Rosilicie Ochoa Bogh is married to a cousin of Assemblyman Russ Bogh (class of 2000), and Assemblywoman Lisa Calderon is the latest member of the Calderon family to be elected. Interestingly, there has been at least one member of the Calderon family in the legislature for nearly forty years, although it was far from clear that would continue when Assembly Majority Leader Ian Calderon announced in 2019 that he would not be seeking reelection. The contentious primary for the seat was between Calderon and Sylvia Rubio, who would have been the third Rubio sister in the legislature.

Assemblymen Thurston Smith and Chris Ward were the first pair of German-born California legislators to arrive in the same class since Assemblymen John D. Siebe and Christian Wentz were elected in 1880.

Also worth noting is Senator Josh Becker's performance in the 2020 election, in which he received more votes than any other first-time legislative candidate in state history.

---

[210] The Assembly Republican caucus grew by one in the 1984 election.

Col. Umberg poses with an artillery piece at Darul Aman Palace (King of Afghanistan Palace) in Kabul, Afghanistan, in 2010.

Courtesy of Senator Tom Umberg

Military Service

> "Liberty is never lost to a nation until it is lost in the souls of the men who compose that nation."
> - *State Senator Nelson S. Dilworth*[211]

Shortly after being elected to his first term in 2010, Assemblyman Jeff Gorell was called to active duty in the U.S. Naval Reserves for a year-long deployment to Afghanistan. Although most didn't realize it, his situation had many similarities to those, seventy years before, of Assemblyman John B. Cooke. In 1940, Cooke was recalled to active duty in the Navy after winning his first Assembly term for a temporary assignment to help run the base at Pearl Harbor. He arrived at Oahu in June, and was present at Pearl Harbor when the Japanese attacked on December 7th.[212]

Gorell and Cooke were only two of a large number of California legislators to go to war. In fact, legislators have fought in almost every U.S. conflict after the American Revolution. In the War of 1812, the conflict in which the British famously burned the White House, Assemblyman Moses Stout was a private in Captain Hale's Company of the Tennessee Militia while Senator Alexander Anderson fought in the Battle of New Orleans.

Jeff Gorell in Afghanistan.
Photo courtesy Jeff Gorell.

---

[211] "What is Our Constitution For?" by Nelson S. Dilworth, from <u>Freedom</u> (CreateSpace Publishing; 2020)
[212] <u>Assembly Daily Journal</u>, 1942 First Extraordinary Session, 19 December 1941, page 4.

During the Civil War, Assemblyman J. Lancaster Brent led Confederate forces in the capture of the Union ironclad USS Indianola and he ended the war as a General. Despite the fame that Brent achieved, many of the California legislators served in the Civil War paid a terrible cost. Senator John T. Crenshaw was killed in a massive explosion during the Battle of Vicksburg, Assemblyman Edward F. W. Ellis was one of nearly 3,500 killed during the Battle of Shiloh, and Assemblyman Truman Reeves lost his left arm at the Battle of Cold Harbor.

Thirty years after the war, a Union Army veteran named Assemblymen William F. Rowell (R-Fresno) learned that his colleague N. L. F. Bachman (D-Fresno) had served in the Confederate Army and that they had fought opposite each other in a number of battles. In spite of their differences, the two became the closest of friends for the rest of their lives[213].

The 1930s saw a large number of veterans of World War I arrive in Sacramento. One of them, Nelson Dilworth, related his experiences and the difficulty describing them to a local civic group;

> "The general subject of the war has been long worn out and I've spent an unhappy week in retrospect of my overseas service. I've tried to forget for years rather than remember...
>
> "Armistice Day was full of surprises, but the saddest was being awakened after nightfall by the steady tramp of men, and discovering that they were Allied soldiers returning from being Prisoners of War. They eagerly ate out of everything in our garbage can, hungry, ragged, with open sores on some, shoeless and crawling with vermin. There were free American men among them who had mothers and [a] home, and in the early morning light there were red stains in the snow where they passed by. I learned again how much I love my native land."[214]

---

[213] History of Fresno County, California (Volume 1) by Paul E. Vandor. page 884. (Historic Record Company, 1919)

[214] "Experiences in France" by Nelson S. Dilworth, Delivered October 3, 1934 at the Hemet Kiwanis Club.

As a legislator, Dilworth frequently returned to this observation in the many speeches he delivered;

> "I feel safe in asserting that it is both obvious and apparent that we, today, are the beneficiaries of the courageous past achievements of our forefathers in political liberty and political institutions... In our hands rests all that is precious in America... We are, you see, the trustees of the future. It is your high privilege to preserve the best in America, to improve it, and pass it on to posterity, your children and mine."[215]

Another veteran of World War I was Willis Winter Bradley, who served aboard the U.S.S. Pittsburgh. In 1917, the ship suffered an accidental ammunition explosion. Bradley, injured in the explosion, crawled into the room where the fire was burning and extinguished it before it could spread to nearby explosives[216]. For his heroism, Bradley was awarded the Medal of Honor by President Coolidge. Assemblyman Bradley remains the only Medal of Honor recipient to serve in the California legislature.

Bradley being awarded the Medal of Honor by President Coolidge. *NH 41628 courtesy of the Naval History & Heritage Command.*

Nearly thirty years later, in the European Theater of World War II, another future legislature would have one of the unique experiences of the war. John A. Busterud arrived on mainland Europe as a junior officer wading ashore at Le Havre three days after his 24th birthday.

In less than a month, Lieutenant Busterud and his company had covered more than 500 miles through France, Luxembourg, and Germany. Near

---

[215] "What is our Constitution for?" from <u>Freedom</u> (CreateSpace; 2020), page 15.
[216] From Bradley's Medal of Honor citation.

the town of Merkers, the arriving troops were told that a huge stockpile of stolen treasure had been hidden deep within a local salt mine. Anticipating sabotage by the retreating German forces, Busterud and his soldiers were sent to the mine to secure it until it could be searched.

When the Army was initially unable to breach a massive steel door to what would later be called "the gold room," it was Busterud's platoon sergeant who had the experience with plastic explosives to finally get through.

This made John Busterud one of the first to see the newly captured 110 tons of gold that made up the complete reserves of the German Reichsbank as well as priceless art and historic artifacts from around the world. In his book Below the Salt, Busterud explained that it was the vast size of the treasure that helped him understand the enemy;

> "With the massive steel door open we took a closer look at the bizarre and depressing scene at the rear of the chamber. The battered valises stored there were crammed full of silver plate and relics, all hammered down to fit into the suitcases. In addition there were countless bags of gold fillings and inlays and many other items of value such as pearls and other precious stones.
>
> "As I viewed this macabre loot collection, I sensed deeply for the first time the kind of regime that had opposed us in the war and the warped mentality of the Nazi leaders and many of their followers as well. As for the vast wealth displayed before us, none of us could comprehend its value in monetary terms. But in any event, we had little free time in which to contemplate the meaning of what our troops had found or to philosophize."[217]

The opening of that vault door was one of the underappreciated turning points in the war. Once it opened, the U.S. Army had full control over the gold that had laid the foundation to the Reichsbank (the equivalent to our Federal Reserve) and German currency. Nazi Germany was no longer

---

[217] Below the Salt by John A. Busterud (Xlibris; 2001), page 114.

in control of its money, and its war machine was rapidly running out of fuel. The German surrender became official a month later.

After returning from the war, Busterud attended law school and moved to California to work as an attorney. He spent the next fifteen years as a legislator writing laws in the Assembly and later as a member of the Constitutional Revision Commission, providing a much needed update to the state constitution.

It's also not just the United States military that California's legislators have served. Even without a declared war, California legislators have demonstrated a willingness to improvise. Henry L. Ford (who would become an Assemblyman in 1851) was one of the thirty-three men who led the Bear Flag Revolt in 1846 by arresting Mexican General (and future State Senator) Mariano G. Vallejo.

Legislators have also participated in their own private wars against our northern and southern neighbors. Twenty years before he was elected to the California State Assembly, Charles Duncombe was forced to flee Canada disguised as a woman after leading a failed armed rebellion against the British Monarchy.

To the south, seven legislators were killed in 1858 when their attempt to incite a revolution in the Mexican state of Sonora failed and the Mexican Army arrived to restore order[218]. Even farther south, two California legislators served as high-ranking officials in the Republic of Nicaragua while the country was occupied in the 1850s by the Private Army of William Walker.

In the current session, the Senate has the larger number of veterans serving, including Army veterans Bob J. Archuleta, Susan T. Eggman, Shannon Grove, Josh Newman, and Tom Umberg as well as Richard Roth (Air Force) and Melissa Melendez (Navy). In the Assembly, veterans include Devon Mathis (Army) and Assemblyman Randy Voepel (Navy).

---

[218] The most former California state legislators to die in a single event was the execution of the Expedition members by the Mexican Army on April 7, 1857.

The grave of Assemblyman Barnabas Collins at Sacramento City Cemetery.

Legislators Who Died in Office

> "The Almighty Giver of all Laws has, in His inscrutable wisdom,
> seen fit to bereave this Assembly of one of its members, and to
> deprive the State of a faithful public servant."
> - *Assemblyman Walter S. Melick speaking about Assemblyman*
> *Barnabas Collins[219]*

When a legislator dies in office, the reminders are everywhere. In the district, a family mourns. In the Chambers, a desk is draped in black. Committees are missing a member, bills are without an author, and staff have to grieve the loss of the boss at the same time as they begin the difficult process of finding a new job. The only good news is that most legislators live for decades after leaving office[220].

Since California became a state, 150 legislators have died in office[221]. The first was State Senator William I. Ferguson, who was fatally wounded in an 1858 duel with former Assemblyman George Pen Johnston. Two years later, John C. Bell became the first Assemblyman to die after he was stabbed by Assemblyman William H. Stone in a fight that erupted during a floor session. The first legislators to die of natural causes were Assemblymembers Thomas Campbell and James Smith in 1862.

Over the years, legislators have died of both routine and unusual causes. Assemblyman Robert W. Crown survived being an infantry rifle platoon leader during World War II but died in 1973 after being struck by a vehicle while out jogging. Senator S. L. Heisinger was killed when his car was struck by a train in 1949 and Assemblyman Alan G. Pattee was killed in a

---

[219] Assembly Daily Journal, 16 January 1901, page 93

[220] The average is 20 years after leaving office, based on 921 known legislators. The longest post-legislative life was George H. Johnson, who lived for 70 years as a former Assemblyman.

[221] An earlier version of this book cited the number as 108 (which remains the official count in the California Blue Book) but excludes a number of legislators who died between the end of the session (the legislature's meetings in Sacramento) but before the end of their elected term.

head-on collision with a drunk driver who had lost control of his pickup truck and crossed into oncoming traffic on Highway 101.

Fortunately, the death of a legislator has become a rare occurrence. In the modern history of the legislature, only six of the 556 legislators who have served since 1991 died in office.

Assemblyman B. T. Collins, who had been severely injured in a grenade blast while serving in Army Special Forces in Vietnam, died of complications of those injuries in 1993. The same year that Collins was wounded in Vietnam, Air Force Major Pete Knight piloted the fastest airplane flight in history in the skies above southern California. Knight was elected to the legislature in 1992 and died while serving in the State Senate in 2004. A year later, Assemblyman Mike Gordon, a well-liked freshman from Los Angeles County, was diagnosed with brain cancer and died three months later after just 202 days in office. Gordon was the youngest legislator to die in office since Assemblyman L. E. Townsend in 1973.

Dave Cox and Jenny Oropeza died in 2010, the first time two senators died in the same year since 1962. First elected to the Assembly in 1998, Cox was an old-fashioned legislator who took more seriously than most the rare honor of evaluating legislation and voting as a representative for hundreds of thousands of his neighbors.

Senator Cox was the last legislator[222] I know of who had a policy of personally returning every call from a constituent who requested it and was the only Assemblymember who didn't miss a single vote on a bill during the two years of the 2000-01 session[223]. After fighting cancer for thirteen years (most of which was during his time in the legislature), Cox died in July 2010.

Senator Jenny Oropeza, a former schoolboard and city councilmember, was diagnosed with cancer five years before while serving in the Assembly. Oropeza died in late October 2010, the first female Senator to die in office, and was reelected to a second term in the election two

---

[222] As far as I'm aware. As of December 2020.
[223] "A Plain Aye or Nay Will Do", Op-Ed, Los Angeles Times, 11 September 2004.

weeks later. Beloved in her district, she has been posthumously honored by the naming of an elementary school, a community center, and parts of two highways in Long Beach for her.

The most recent legislator to die in office was Senator Sharon Runner in 2016. In her sixth and final year in the Assembly, Runner announced that she was being put on a list to receive a lung transplant because limited scleroderma was causing thickening of her lung tissue. In spite of this, Runner ran for a state Senate vacancy in 2011 after her husband resigned following his election to the state Board of Equalization.

Almost exactly a year into her first term in the Senate, Runner became the first known double-lung transplant survivor to serve in a state legislature. On the advice of doctors, who encouraged her to limit exposure to the public, she announced shortly after that she would not be seeking reelection because of her health.

Two years later, when her successor was elected to Congress, Runner again campaigned for the Senate and became the first person ever elected to the State Senate twice in special elections as well as only the third legislator in the previous fifty years to serve non-consecutive terms in the Senate. Runner served a little less than a year and a half of her second term in the Senate before her death in July 2016.

There have also been eight individuals elected to the legislature who died before assuming office[224]. Fortunately, we haven't had a legislator die before assuming office in well over a century.

---

[224] These eight were Senators-elect George W. Seaton in 1865 and Charles L. Pond in 1890 as well as Assemblymembers-elect L. Dunlap in 1850, James H. Carson in 1853, Thomas Robertson in 1859, W. J. Maclay in 1879, William L. Morton in 1882, and J. H. Krimminger in 1904.

Even before serving in the first session of the state legislature, Mariano G. Vallejo had served for years in the administration of California. He began as the secretary to Governor Argüello while California was still part of Spain (1825), became the highest ranking military officer in the province as well as a member of the territorial legislature during the Mexican era (1831-1846), finally served as a delegate to the state's first constitutional convention (1849) during the early American period.

The USS Vallejo, named for the General, carried sixteen ballistic missiles with nuclear warheads, providing a significant part of the U.S. nuclear deterrent during the second half of the Cold War (1966-1995). Since the decommissioning of the Vallejo, her conning tower has been displayed on Mare Island.

Named for a Legislator

"I hope some bird will catch this Grub the next time he calls Lake Bigler by so disgustingly sick and silly a name as 'Lake Tahoe."
– Mark Twain[225]

Sometimes, the source of a place name is fairly well known, like the City of Vallejo being named for the General who owned the land and laid out the plans for that city. Other names, like those of mountains and lakes[226], can be largely lost to time. Sometimes, as with Denver, Colorado, it takes a longer explanation to understand why another state's largest city is named for a California legislator.

Denver came to California as a soldier during the Mexican-American War and was elected to the State Senate in 1852. Shortly after his election, he was challenged to a duel by Congressman Edward Gilbert who had been offended by an article Denver wrote. During the first round, Denver fired his rifle into the air while Gilbert aimed at him and missed. Denver tried to call off a second round, but Gilbert refused, demanding another attempt to shoot him.

Unable to avoid a second round and understanding that Gilbert wanted to kill him, Denver shot and killed Gilbert in the second round[227]. Six months later, Denver was appointed Secretary of State. In 1857, Denver moved to the Territory of Kansas, where he was elected Governor within months. During his tenure as Governor, the city of Denver was founded and named for him.

---

[225] The Works of Mark Twain; Early Tales & Sketches, Vol. 1 (1851-1864), (UC Press; 1979), page 290.

[226] The primary sources for this section are California Place Names by Erwin G. Gudde (University of California Press; 2010) and 2019 Named Freeways, Highways, Structures and Other Appurtenances in California by Caltrans (2020).

[227] Choose Your Weapon: The Duel in California by Christopher Burchfield (Stairway Press; 2013), pp. 72-74.

Unfortunately, there is always an inherent danger in naming places after living people; that they will do something that puts the locals in the difficult position of either continuing to live with the sullied name or asking for a new name (which I imagine would bring a great deal of embarrassment to the formerly honored individual). This was the case with Lake Bigler, named in 1853 for an assemblyman from the first legislature who became Governor in 1851[228].

Public acceptance of his name on California's largest lake declined in the 1860s, when Bigler supported the Confederacy during the Civil War. By the end of the 1870s, common usage of the name "Lake Bigler" had ended. It wasn't until 1945 that the name was officially changed to Lake Tahoe, leaving only a cautionary tale about naming things too soon.

There are events that nobody wants named after them. After serving in the Assembly in 1861, Magruder moved to Idaho and started a business transporting supplies by pack-train to mines in Montana. Returning from a successful trip, during which he had collected nearly a hundred pounds of gold dust, Magruder and four others were murdered during a robbery.[229] The "Magruder Massacre" has lent its name to the nearby 101-mile long Magruder Corridor Road and Magruder Campground.

---

[228] It was Governor Bigler who appointed Denver as Secretary of State in 1853.
[229] This Bloody Deed: The Magruder Incident by Ladd Hamilton (Washington State University Press; 1994)

Lakes, Creeks, and Hot Springs

John Bigler	Lake Bigler [Placer and El Dorado Co.] *(Officially renamed Lake Tahoe in 1945)*
Lewis R. Bradley	Bradley Creek [Elko County, Nevada]
Prescott F. Cogswell	Cogswell Reservoir [Los Angeles Co.]
C. F. Curry	Lake Curry [Napa Co.]
James F. Cunningham	Lake Cunningham [Santa Clara Co.]
Lester T. Davis	Lake Davis [Plumas Co.]
James G. Denniston	Denniston Creek [San Mateo Co.]
Clair Engle	Clair Engle Lake [Trinity Co.] *(Renamed Trinity Lake in 1997)*
Lloyd Magruder	Magruder Creek [Idaho]
Gwen Moore	Gwen Moore Lake [Los Angeles Co.]
William W. Stow	Stow Lake [San Francisco Co.]
Jonathan T. Warner	Warner Hot Springs [San Diego Co.]

Mineral

William T. Coleman	Colemanite *A borate combining borax and ulexite*

Hollister Peak in San
Luis Obispo County.

Mountains, Peaks, Hills, and Passes

John Conness   Mt. Conness   [Mono/Tuolumne Co.; 12,649']

William McConnell McConnell Peak   [El Dorado Co.; 9,099']

James N. Gillett   Gillette Mountain [Tuolumne Co.; 8,291']

John Bidwell   Mt. Bidwell   [Modoc Co.; 8,266']

David C. Broderick Mt. Broderick   [Mariposa Co.; 6,696']

B. D. Wilson   Mt. Wilson   [Los Angeles Co.; 5,712']

John G. Downey   Downey Peak   [Orange Co., 5,689'][230]

James H. Hollister Hollister Peak   [San Luis Obispo Co.; 1,404']

James Smith   Smith Mountain   [Fresno Co.; 1,017']

D. N. Sherburne   Sherburne Hills   [Contra Costa Co.; 850']

Edward Fletcher   Fletcher Hills   [San Diego Co.; 833']

John Daggett   Daggett Pass   [Alpine Co.]

---

[230] <u>California Place Names</u> by Erwin Gudde (UC Press, 1969), page 93.

Fire Station #1 in the
City of Hollister

Cities and Towns

Thomas Baker	Bakersfield [Kern Co.]
Phineas Banning	Banning [Riverside Co.]
John Bidwell	Fort Bidwell [Modoc Co.]
	Bidwell Bar [Butte Co.] *(Under Lake Oroville since 1968)*
Marion Biggs	Biggs [Butte Co.]
Sam Brannan	Brannan Springs [Alpine Co.] *(Renamed Woodfords)*
David C. Broderick	Broderick [Yolo Co.] *(Now part of West Sacramento)*
James H. Carson	Carson Hill [Calaveras Co.]
John Daggett	Daggett [San Bernardino Co.]
James A. Denver	Denver [Denver Co., Colorado] Denverton [Solano Co.]
John G. Downey	Downey [Los Angeles Co.]
Charles S. Fairfax	Fairfax [Marin Co.]
Charles N. Felton	Felton [Santa Cruz Co.]
Thomas Fowler	Fowler [Fresno Co.]
Harmon G. Heald	Healdsburg [Sonoma Co.]
The Hollister Family J. J. "Jim" Hollister Sr. J. J. "Jack" Hollister Jr.	Hollister [San Benito Co.] Hollister Ranch [San Benito Co.]

"Welcome to Watsonville"
Photo Courtesy Mike Vassar

Daniel Inman	Danville [Contra Costa Co.]
Julius M. Keeler	Keeler [Inyo Co.]
Benjamin B. Redding	Redding [Shasta Co.]
Charles Robinson	Robinson, Kansas
James Smith	Smith's Ferry [Fresno Co.] *(Renamed Reedley in 1870s)*
L. G. Smith	Smithville [Placer Co.] *(Renamed Loomis in 1890)*
Philip A. Stanton	Stanton [Orange Co.]
Mariano G. Vallejo	Vallejo [Solano Co.]
Jonathan T. Warner	Warner Springs [San Diego Co.]
John H. Watson	Watsonville [Santa Cruz Co.]
Abner Weed	Weed [Siskiyou Co.]

Neighborhoods

Newton Booth	Newton Booth Neighborhood (Sacramento)
Edward R. Amerige	Amerige Heights Neighborhood (Fullerton)

U.S. Naval Vessels

Selim E. Woodworth

USS Woodworth (DD-460)
Benson-class destroyer (1941-1952)

Willis W. Bradley

USS Bradley (DE 1041 and FF 1041)
Garcia-class Destroyer Escort (1965-1975)
Garcia-class Frigate (1975-1988)

Mariano G. Vallejo

USS Mariano G. Vallejo (SSBN 658)
Franklin-class Missile Submarine (1966-1995)

Glenard P. Lipscomb

USS Glenard P. Lipscomb (SSN-685)
Lipscomb-class Attack Submarine (1974-1990)

Federal Buildings[231]

Glenn M. Anderson
Glenn M. Anderson Federal Building
Long Beach

Phil Burton
Phillip Burton Federal Building and Courthouse
San Francisco

B. T. Collins
B.T. Collins U.S. Army Reserve Center
Sacramento

B.T. Collins High Tech Training Center
Sacramento

William B. Rumford
William Byron Rumford Post Office
Oakland

Leo J. Ryan
Leo J. Ryan Memorial Federal Building
San Mateo

Leo J. Ryan Post Office
San Mateo

John E. Moss
John E. Moss Federal Building and Courthouse
Sacramento

John Bidwell
Fort Bidwell (1865-1890)
Modoc County

Camp Bidwell (1863-1865)[232]
Butte County

---

[231] "Key GSA-Owned Facilities in California" accessed on 27 December 2020 at http://www.gsa.gov/portal/category/22381

[232] Camp Bidwell was renamed Camp Chico in 1865 and remained in service until 1893.

The Department of Corrections and Rehabilitation's Deuel Vocational Institution in Tracy.

DEUEL
VOCATIONAL
INSTITUTION

CALIFORNIA PRISON INDUSTRY

DEUEL VOCATIONAL INSTITUTION

State Buildings/Facilities

Al Alquist — Alquist State Office Building (San Jose)

Hugh M. Burns — Hugh Burns State Building (Fresno)

B. T. Collins — B.T. Collins California Conservation Corps Building (Sacramento)

Wadie P. Deddeh — Wadie P. Deddeh State Office Building (San Diego)

Charles H. Deuel — Deuel Vocational Institution (Tracy)

Richard J. Donovan — Richard Donovan Correctional Facility (San Diego)

Donovan Correctional Facility (Rock Mountain)

March Fong Eu — March Fong Eu Secretary of State Building (Sacramento)

Elihu Harris — Elihu M Harris State Office Building (Oakland)

Pete Knight — Pete Knight Veterans Home of CA (Palmdale)

Frank D. Lanterman — Lanterman Developmental Center (Pomona)

James R. Mills — James R. Mills State Office Building (San Diego)

E. M. Preston — Preston School of Industry (Ione)

Joseph A. Rattigan — Judge Joseph A. Rattigan Building (Santa Rosa)

Stephen P. Teale — Stephen P. Teale Data Center Gold Campus (Rancho Cordova)

Jesse M. Unruh — Jesse Unruh State Office Building (Sacramento)

Eshleman Hall on the UC Berkeley campus.

State Buildings (Colleges and University)

Samuel H. Beckett   Beckett Hall[233]
UC Davis

Willie Brown   Willie L. Brown, Jr. Leadership Center
San Francisco State University

Pedro C. Carrillo   Carrillo Hall
UC Santa Barbara

Pablo De La Guerra   De La Guerra Dining Commons
Antonio De La Guerra   *UC Santa Barbara*

Earl D. Desmond   Desmond Hall (Residence Hall)
CSU Sacramento

Ralph C. Dills   Dills Vocational Technology Center
El Camino College

Julian C. Dixon   Julian C. Dixon Courtroom and Advocacy Center
Southwestern Law School

Dorothy M. Donahoe   Donahoe Hall
CSU Bakersfield

John W. Dwinelle   Dwinelle Hall
UC Berkeley

Mervyn Dymally   Mervyn M. Dymally School of Nursing
Charles Drew University

John M. Eshleman   Eshleman Hall
UC Berkeley

John Morton Eshleman Library
UC Berkeley

---

[233] No longer exists.

State Buildings (Colleges and University)

Edward Fletcher   Fletcher Chimes (in Hardy Memorial Tower)
San Diego State University

George Hearst   Hearst Memorial Mining Building
UC Berkeley

Ken Maddy   Kenneth L. Maddy Institute
CSU Fresno

Maddy Equine Analytical Chemistry Laboratory
UC Davis

Leo T. McCarthy   Leo T. McCarthy Center for Public Service
University of San Francisco

Nicholas C. Petris   Petris Center on Health Care Markets and
Consumer Welfare
UC Berkeley

Alfred W. Robertson   Robertson Gymnasium "Rob Gym"
UC Santa Barbara

Albert S. Rodda   Rodda Hall
Sacramento City College

Charles A. Storke   Storke Tower
UC Santa Barbara

Jesse M. Unruh   Unruh Institute of Politics
University of Southern California

Parks, Beaches, and Wildlife Areas

Richard Alatorre Richard Alatorre Park (Los Angeles)

Edward R. Amerige Amerige Park (Fullerton)

Mike Antonovich Antonovich Open Space Preserve (Los Angeles Co.)

Ruben S. Ayala Ayala Park (San Bernardino Co.)
Ayala Park (Chino)

John Bidwell Bidwell Mansion State Historic Park (Chico)
Bidwell-Sacramento River State Park (near Chico)
Bidwell River Park (Chico)
Bidwell Park (Chico)
Bidwell Park (Hayward)
Bidwell Municipal Golf Course (Chico)

David C. Broderick Broderick Boat Ramp (West Sacramento)

Phil Burton Phillip Burton Memorial Beach (San Mateo Co.)

Burton W. Chace Burton W. Chace Park (Marina del Rey)

W. F. Chandler Chandler Park (Fresno)

B. T. Collins B. T. Collins Park (Folsom)

Robert W. Crown Robert W. Crown Mem. State Beach (Alameda)

Pablo De la Guerra De la Guerra Plaza (Santa Barbara)
Antonio M. De la Guerra

Ralph C. Dills Ralph C. Dills Park (Paramount)

Victor Fazio, Jr. Vic Fazio Yolo Wildlife Area (Yolo Co.)

Robert Frazee Frazee State Beach (Carlsbad)

Joe A. Gonsalves Joe A. Gonsalves Park (Cerritos)

Parks, Beaches, and Wildlife Areas (continued)

Augustus F. Hawkins Augustus F. Hawkins Natural Park (Los Angeles)

Harold T. Johnson Bizz Johnson National Recreation Trail
(Lassen Co.)
Home of the "Bizz Johnson Marathon"

George Miller Miller/Knox Regional Shoreline (Alameda Co.)
John T. Knox

Culbert L. Olson Culbert Olson Redwood Grove (Humboldt Co.)

Andres Pico Andres Pico Adobe Park (Los Angeles Co.)

John P. Quimby John Quimby Park (Los Angeles)

Leo J. Ryan Leo J. Ryan Park (Foster City)

Alan Sieroty Alan Sieroty Beach (Marin Co.)

Sally Tanner Sally Tanner Park (Los Angeles)

John E. Thurman Jr. John Thurman [Athletic] Field (Modesto, CA)

Arthur W. Way Arthur W. Way County Memorial Park
(Humboldt Co.)

Edwin L. Z'berg Ed Z'berg - Sugar Pine Point State Park
(Lake Tahoe)

Auditoriums, Performing Arts, and Community Centers

Anthony Beilenson Anthony C. Beilenson Visitor Center
(Thousand Oaks)

Marian C. Bergeson Marian Bergeson Aquatic Center
(Newport Beach)

Jim Brulte James L. Brulte Senior Center
(Rancho Cucamonga)

The Romero Visitors Center on a hillside above the San Luis Reservoir.

Larry Chimbole	Larry Chimbole Cultural Center (Palmdale)
B. T. Collins	B.T. Collins Juvenile Center (Sacramento)
Delaine Eastin	Delaine Eastin Daycare Center (Fremont)
Augustus Hawkins	Hawkins Mental Health Center (Los Angeles)
Nate Holden	Nate Holden Performing Arts Center (Los Angeles)
Thomas H. Kuchel	Thomas Kuchel Visitor Center (Redwood National Park)
Sheila Kuehl	Sheila Kuehl Family Wellness Center (San Fernando)
Abel Maldonado	Maldonado Community Youth Center (Santa Maria)
Bruce McPherson	McPherson Center for Art and History (Santa Cruz)
Henry Mello	Mello Center for the Performing Arts (Watsonville)
Juanita Millender-McDonald	Congresswoman Juanita Millender-McDonald Community Center (Carson)
George R. Moscone	Moscone Recreation Center (San Francisco) Moscone Convention Center (San Francisco)
George Nakano	George Nakano Theatre (Torrance)
Jenny Oropeza	Jenny Oropeza Community Center (Long Beach)
Gloria Romero	Romero Visitors Center (San Luis Reservoir)
Alan Short	Alan Short Center (Stockton)
Curtis R. Tucker	Curtis R. Tucker Health Center (Inglewood)

The Terminal of Fresno Chandler Executive Airport. *Photo courtesy John Chandler.*

Airports[234]

W. F. Chandler   Fresno Chandler Executive Airport
                         Fresno, CA

John Daggett   Barstow-Daggett Airport Daggett
                         San Bernardino Co.

James W. Denver   Denver International Airport
                         Denver Co., Colorado

John Bidwell   Fort Bidwell Airport
                         Modoc Co.

Boats and Ships

William Irwin   Governor Irwin [fireboat]
                         San Francisco Fire Department (1878-1909)

John A. McClelland[235]   J. A. McClelland [Stern-wheel steamer]
                         Steam Navigation Company (1860-1861)

Benches

Bob Moretti   Bob Moretti Memorial Bench
                         Capitol Park, Sacramento

Sharon Runner   Sharon Runner Memorial Bench
                         Capitol Park, Sacramento

---

[234] All airports on this list except for Chandler are actually named for the nearby town, which was named for the legislator. Chandler Airport is named for the Senator, who donated family land for the construction of the facility.

[235] "A Steamer's History", Sacramento Daily Union, 29 January 1873, page 3. California Digital Newspaper Collection. Web. Accessed 12 December 2016

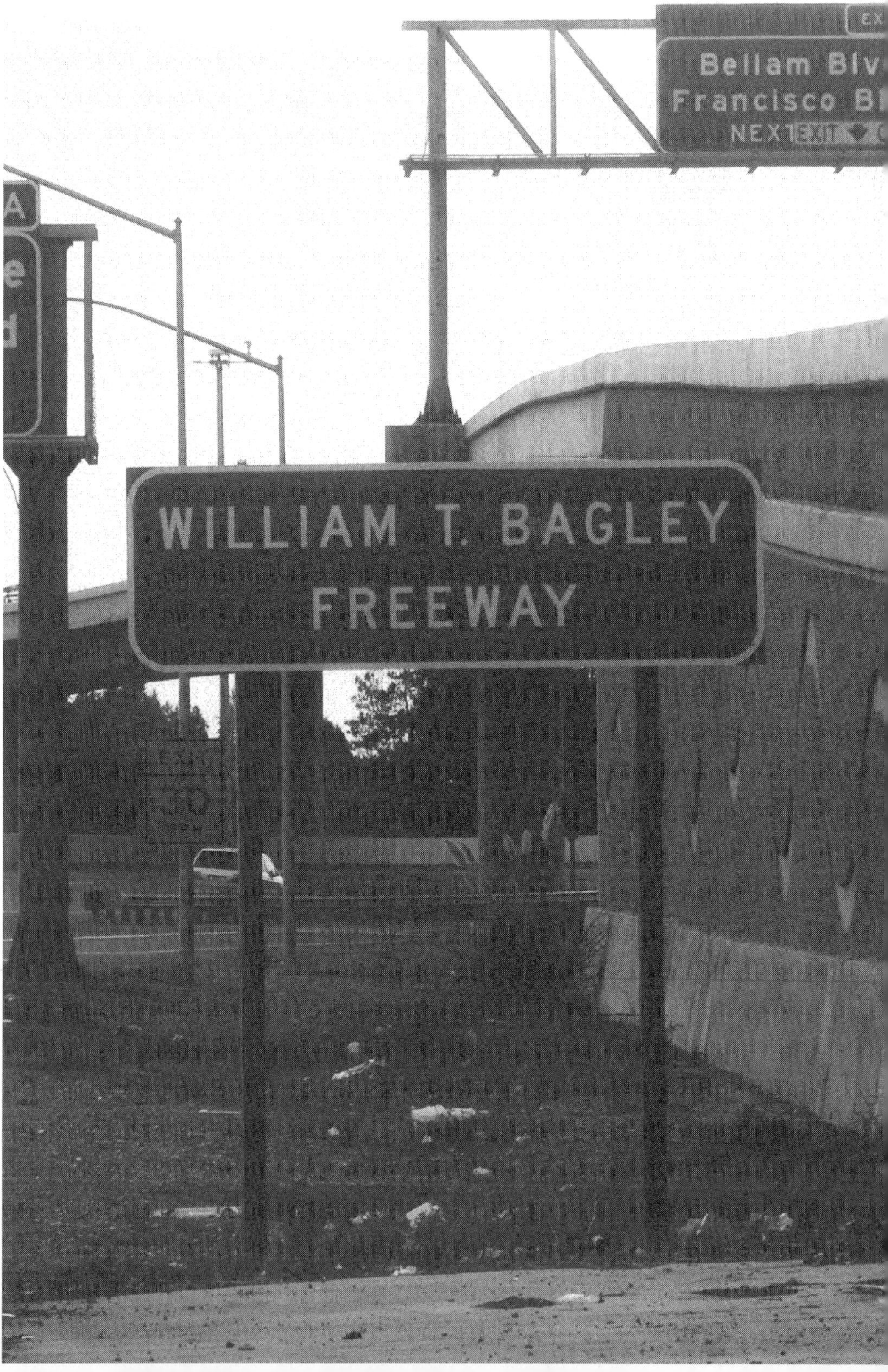
WILLIAM T. BAGLEY
FREEWAY

Freeways and Highways

Glenn M. Anderson
Glenn Anderson Freeway
State Route 105 in Los Angeles Co.

Bill Bagley
William T. Bagley Freeway
US 101 in San Rafael

Frank P. Belotti
Frank P. Belotti Freeway
US 101 in Humboldt Co.
Frank P. Belotti Memorial Freeway
US 101 in Humboldt Co.

John C. Begovich
John C. Begovich Memorial Highway
State Route 49 in Amador Co.

Dan Boatwright
Senator Daniel E. Boatwright Highway
I-680 in Contra Costa Co.

Charles Brown
Charles Brown Highway
State Route 178 in Inyo Co.

George Brown
George E. Brown Memorial Freeway
I-210 in San Bernardino Co.

Gene Chappie
Eugene "Gene" Chappie Memorial Highway
State Route 193 in El Dorado Co.

Larry Chimbole
Larry Chimbole Memorial Highway
State Route 138 in Los Angeles Co.

Dave Cogdill
Senator David E. Cogdill, Sr., Memorial Highway
State Route 395 in Mono Co.

Jim Costa
Senator Jim Costa Highway
State Route 180 in Fresno Co.

Donald D. Doyle
Donald D. Doyle Highway
I- 680 in Contra Costa Co.

Vic Fazio
Vic Fazio Highway
State Route 113 in Sacramento Co.

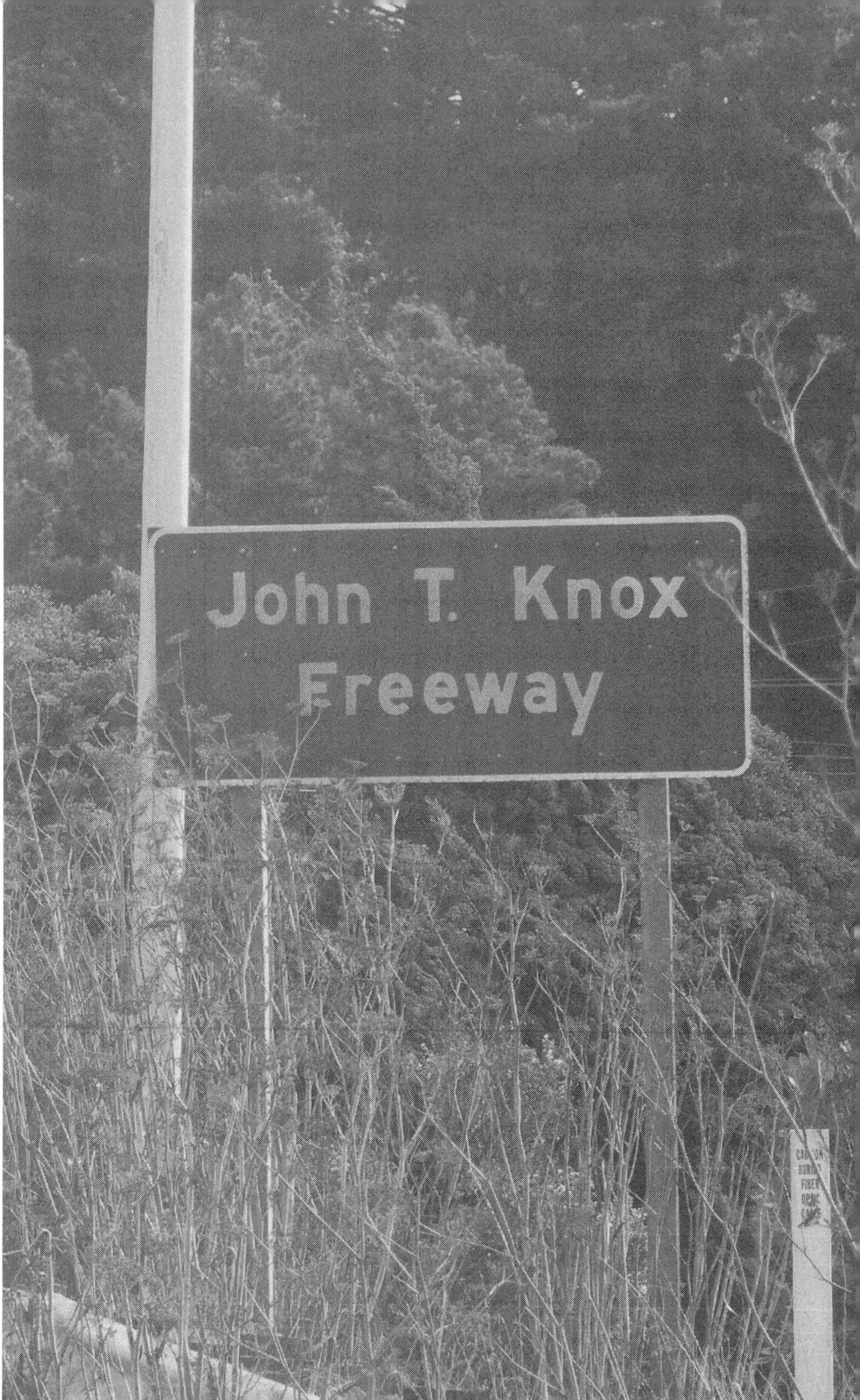
John T. Knox
Freeway

John Francis Foran	John F. Foran Freeway *I-280 in San Francisco Co.*
Luther Gibson	Luther Gibson Freeway *I-680 in Solano Co.*
Ben Hulse	Ben Hulse Highway *State Route 78 in Imperial Co.*
Harold T. Johnson	Harold T. 'Bizz' Johnson Expressway *State Route 65 in Placer Co.*
David G. Kelley	Senator David G. Kelley Highway *State Route 86 in Riverside Co.*
John T. Knox	John T. Knox Freeway *I-580 in Contra Costa Co.*
Quentin L. Kopp	Quentin L. Kopp Freeway *I-380 in San Mateo Co.*
Frank D. Lanterman	Frank D. Lanterman Freeway *State Route 2 in Los Angeles Co.*
Paul J. Lunardi	Paul J. Lunardi Memorial Highway *State Route 267 in Placer Co.*
Ken Maddy	Kenneth L. Maddy Freeway *State Route 99 in Merced Co.*
Henry Mello	Senator Henry J. Mello Highway *State Route 1 in Monterey Co.*
Bob Monagan	Robert T. Monagan Freeway *I-205 in San Joaquin Co.*
Willard H. Murray Jr.	Willard H. Murray Freeway *State Route 91 in Los Angeles Co.*
Robert Nimmo	Robert and Pat Nimmo Memorial Highway *State Route 41 in San Luis Obispo Co.*

Jack O'Connell   Jack O'Connell Highway
State Route 46 in San Luis Obispo Co.

Jenny Oropeza   Senator Jenny Oropeza Memorial Freeway
State Route 710 in Long Beach

Lou Papan   Louis J. Papan Highway
Highway 1 in San Mateo Co.

Chuck Poochigian   Senator Chuck Poochigian Highway
State Route 180 in Fresno Co.

Bernie Richter   Bernie Richter Memorial Highway
Highway 99 in Sutter Co.

Sharon Runner   Sharon Runner Memorial Highway
State Highway Route 14 in Los Angeles Co.

William B. Rumford   William Byron Rumford Freeway
State Route 24 in Alameda Co.

Eric Seastrand   Eric Seastrand Memorial Highway
State Route 46 in San Luis Obispo Co.

Vernon L. Sturgeon   Vernon L. Sturgeon Memorial Highway
US 101 in San Luis Obispo Co.

Stephen P. Teale   Stephen P. Teale Highway
State Route 26 in Calaveras Co.

Victor V. Veysey   Victor V. Veysey Expressway
State Route 78 in Brawley, CA

John G. Veneman   John Veneman Freeway
Highway 99 near Modesto, CA

Clarence C. Ward   Clarence Ward Memorial Boulevard
State Route 217 in Santa Barbara

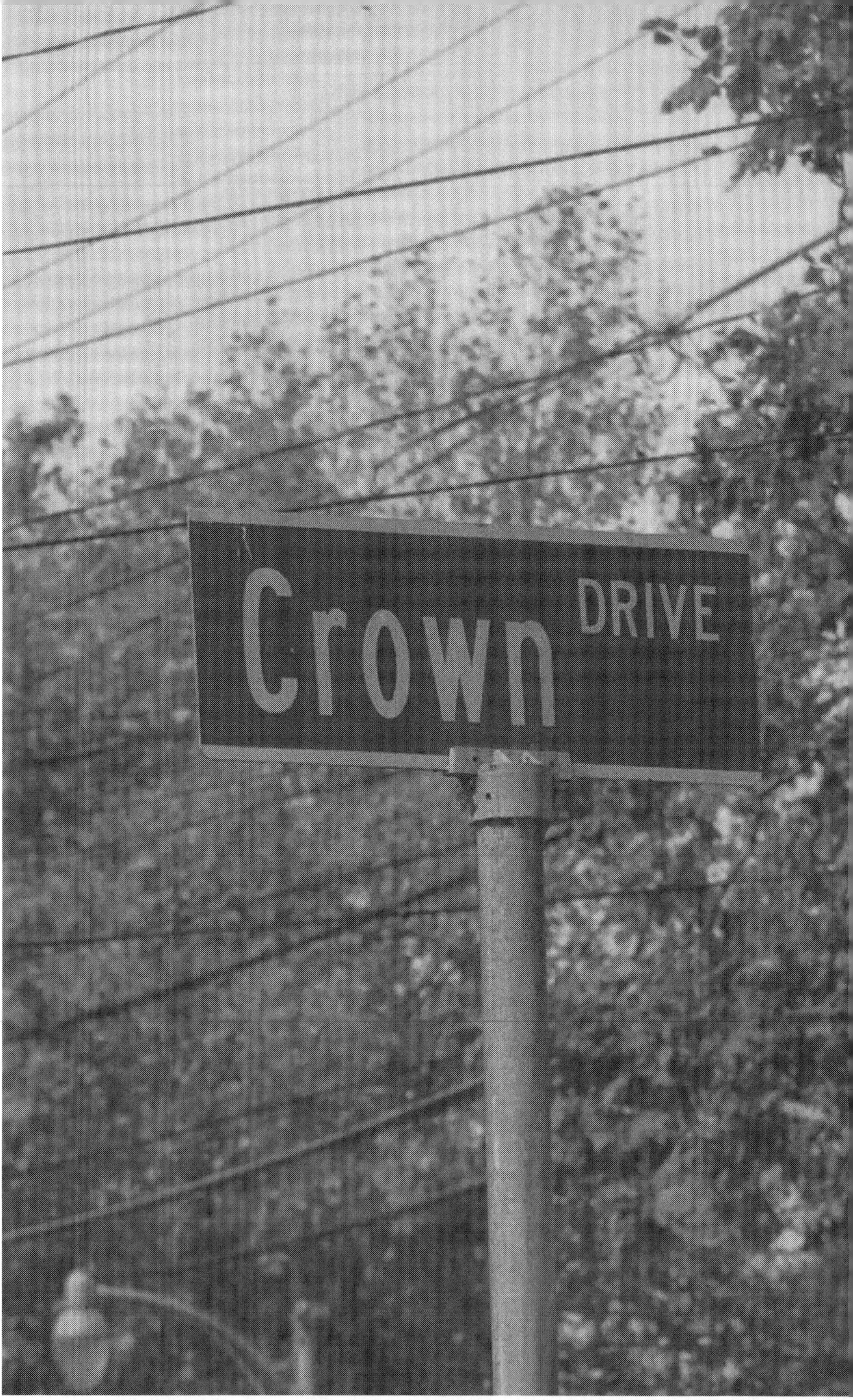
Crown DRIVE

Streets, Roads, and Avenues

Carlisle Abbott   Abbott Street (Salinas)

Edward R. Amerige   Amerige Avenue (Fullerton)

Ruben S. Ayala   Ayala Drive (Rialto)

John Bidwell   Bidwell Way (Sacramento)
Bidwell Way (Vallejo)
Bidwell Avenue (Chico)

Samuel Brannan   Brannan Street (San Francisco)

David C. Broderick   Broderick Street (San Francisco)

W. F. Chandler   Chandler Street (Selma)
Chandler Avenue (Fresno)

John Conness   Conness Way (Sacramento)

Ernest C. Crowley   Crowley Lane (Fairfield)

Antonio De la Guerra   Antonio De la Guerra Place (Santa Barbara)
Pablo De la Guerra   De la Guerra Road (Santa Barbara)
De la Guerra Street (Santa Barbara)
De la Guerra Terrace (Santa Barbara)

George Deukmejian   Deukmejian Drive (Long Beach)

Edward F. W. Ellis   Ellis Street (San Francisco)

Robert Frazee   Frazee Road (San Luis Rey Valley)

John B. Frisbie   Frisbie Street (Vallejo)

Charles H. Gough   Gough Street (San Francisco)

Isadore Hall   Isadore Hall Drive (Compton)

Horace Hawes   Hawes Street (San Francisco)

John J. Hollister	Hollister Avenue (Goleta)
Lloyd Magruder Jr.	The Magruder Corridor *A 101-mile road through Idaho and Montana*
Timothy G. Phelps	Phelps Street (San Francisco)
Leander Quint	Quint Street (San Francisco)
James P. Sargent	Sargent Street (Gilroy) *[Renamed First Street in the 1860s]*
John F. Shelley	John F. Shelley Drive (San Francisco)
William M. Steuart	Steuart Street (San Francisco)
Mariano G. Vallejo	Vallejo Avenue (Inverness) Vallejo Avenue (Novato) Vallejo Avenue (Rodeo) Vallejo Avenue (Roseville) Vallejo Avenue (Sonoma) Vallejo Court (Millbrae) Vallejo Court (French Camp) Vallejo Drive (Millbrae) Vallejo Drive (Orangevale) Vallejo Street (Crockett) Vallejo Street (Emeryville) Vallejo Street (Napa) Vallejo Street (Petaluma) Vallejo Street (San Francisco) Vallejo Way (Fremont) Vallejo Way (Sacramento) Vallejo Way (San Rafael)
James P. Van Ness	Van Ness Avenue (San Francisco)
John G. Veneman	Veneman Avenue (Modesto)
William T. Wallace	Wallace Street (San Francisco)

Interchanges and Bridges

Frank P. Belotti
Frank P. Belotti Memorial Bridge
US 101 over the Eel River

John Bidwell
Bidwell Bar Bridge
State Route 162 in Butte Co.

Carl Christensen Jr.
Carl L. Christensen Memorial Bridge
State Route 255 in Humboldt Co.

Randolph Collier
Randolph Collier Tunnel
US 199 near the Oregon State Line

Dave Cox
Senator Dave Cox Memorial Interchange
Highway 50 at Hazel Avenue in Sacramento Co.

Joe A. Gonsalves
Joe A. Gonsalves Memorial Interchange
I-105/I-605

Jack Hollister Jr.
Senator John J. Hollister Memorial Bridge
State Route 166 in San Luis Obispo Co.

Harold T. Johnson
Harold "Bizz" Johnson Interchange
State Route 92/US 101 in San Mateo Co.

James J. McBride
Senator James J. McBride Memorial Bridge
US 101 in Ventura Co.

Jack McCarthy
John F. McCarthy Memorial Bridge
I-580 at San Rafael Bay

John Nejedly
Senator John A. Nejedly Bridge
State Route 160 at the Sacramento Delta

Jenny Oropeza
Honorable Jenny Oropeza Memorial
Overcrossing
State Route 1 in Los Angeles Co.

Jack Schrade
Jack Schrade Bridge
I- 805 in San Diego Co.

View of Donner Lake from McGlashan Point near Truckee. *Photo courtesy Richard Paul.*

McGLASHAN POINT
DEDICATED AUGUST 10, 1986 IN HONOR OF
CHARLES FAYETTE McGLASHAN
1847 — 1931
TRUCKEE'S PATRIARCH, HISTORIAN, AUTHOR, EDITOR

Vincent Thomas Vincent Thomas Memorial Bridge
State Route 47 in Los Angeles Co.

Rose Ann Vuich Rose Ann Vuich Interchange
State Route 41 and State Route 180

Rest Areas[236]

Randolph Collier Randolph E. Collier (Klamath) Rest Area
Interstate 5 in Siskiyou Co.

Lester Davis Lester T. Davis Rest Area
State Route 70 in Plumas Co.

Elmer S. Rigdon Rigdon Drinking Fountain
Highway 1 in Monterey Co.

Abner Weed Weed Rest Area
I-5 in Siskiyou Co.

Scenic Overlook

Charles F. McGlashan McGlashan Point
Donner Summit near Truckee

Traffic Circle

Willie L. Brown, Jr. Willie L. Brown, Jr. Circle and Plaza
900 Block of Capitol Mall, Sacramento

---

[236] 2019 Named Freeways, Highways, Structures and Other Appurtenances in California by the California Department of Transportation (2020)

High Schools[237]

Ruben S. Ayala	Ruben S. Ayala High School (Chino Hills)
John Bidwell	Bidwell Continuation High School (Antioch)
Phil Burton	Phillip and Sala Burton Academic High School (San Francisco)
Wilmer Amina Carter	Wilmer Amina Carter High School (Rialto)
Marco A. Firebaugh	Marco Antonio Firebaugh High School (Lynwood)
Pete Knight	William J. "Pete" Knight High School (Palmdale)
Frank D. Lanterman	F. D. Lanterman High School (Los Angeles)
Gene McAteer	J. Eugene McAteer High School (San Francisco)
John A. O'Connell	John O'Connell High School of Technology (San Francisco)
Jenny Oropeza	Jenny Oropeza Global Studies Academy Jenny Oropeza Elementary School (Long Beach)

Middle Schools

John Bidwell	Bidwell Junior High School (Chico)
Willie Brown	Willie Brown Jr. Middle School (San Francisco)
Leroy F. Greene	Leroy Greene Academy (Sacramento)[238]

---

[237] George S. Patton Continuation High School (in Los Angeles) is named for the military General, not his father the Assemblyman.

[238] Previously operated as the Leroy F. Greene Middle School from 1994 to 2010.

Elementary Schools

Marian C. Bergeson   Marian Bergeson Elementary School
(Laguna Niguel)

John Bidwell   Bidwell Elementary School (Antioch)

Bidwell Elementary School (Sacramento)

Bidwell Elementary School (Red Bluff)

Benjamin Corey   Benjamin Cory Elementary School (San Jose)

Nelson S. Dilworth   Nelson S. Dilworth Elementary (San Jose)

Delaine Eastin   Delaine Eastin Elementary School (Union City)

Edward F. W. Ellis   Ellis Elementary and Art Alternative School
(Rockford, Illinois)

Joe A. Gonsalves   Joe A. Gonsalves Elementary School (Cerritos)

George Hearst   Hearst Elementary (San Diego)

Ben Hulse   Ben Hulse Elementary School (Imperial)

Teresa Hughes   Teresa Hughes Elementary School (Cudahy)

John G. Mattos Jr.   John G. Mattos Elementary (Fremont)

John J. McFall   John J. McFall School (Manteca)

George R. Moscone   George Moscone Elementary School
(San Francisco)

Frank Otis   Frank Otis Elementary School (Alameda)

William F. Prisk   William F. Prisk Elementary School (Long Beach)

B. D. Wilson   Don Benito Elementary School (Pasadena)

The Rose Ann Vuich Hearing Room
(State Capitol, Room 2040)

Rooms, Offices, and Suites

Willie Brown
Willie Brown Conference Room
California State Capitol, Room 223

Al Alquist
Al Alquist Budget Suite
California State Capitol, Room 5019

Tom Bane
Tom Bane Assembly Rules Committee Room
California State Capitol, Room 3162

John Burton
John Burton Hearing Room
California State Capitol, Room 4203

Dave Cox
Cox's Club House [Republican Caucus Room]
California State Capitol, Near Room 3044

Bill Leonard
Bill Leonard Training Room
Legislative Office Building, Room 375

Ken Maddy
Maddy Lounge [Democratic Caucus Room]
California State Capitol, Room 3030

Milton Marks
Milton Marks Conference Center
State Office Building in San Francisco

Anthony Pescetti
Anthony Pescetti Community Room
Galt Police Station

Nicholas C. Petris
Senator Nicholas Petris Room (Room 3023)
Sacramento State University Library

Jesse M. Unruh
Jesse Unruh Hearing Room
California State Capitol, Room 4202

Rose Ann Vuich
Rose Ann Vuich Hearing Room
California State Capitol, Rooms 2040

Rose Room
California State Capitol, Rooms 3169

Programs, Institutes, and Awards

Marian C. Bergeson Marian Bergeson Award
Orange County School Boards Association

Lewis Dan Bohnett Willow Glen Founder's Day
Willow Glen Neighborhood in San Jose, CA

George Brown Jr. George E. Brown, Jr., Salinity Laboratory
Riverside Co.

Jim Brulte James L. Brulte Fellowship
UC Irvine

B. T. Collins B.T. Collins "Captain Hook" Scholarship[239]
Santa Clara University

Julian C. Dixon Julian C. Dixon Institute for Cultural Studies
Los Angeles, CA
Julian Dixon Library
Culver City, CA

John Foran John F. Foran Legislative Award
Metropolitan Transportation Commission

Gary K. Hart Hart Vision Award
California Charter Schools Association

Bob Hertzberg Robert M. Hertzberg Capitol Institute
California State Assembly

Bob Hertzberg
Gray Davis Hertzberg-Davis Forensic Science Center
Los Angeles, CA

Robert Kirkwood Robert C. Kirkwood [Hydroelectric] Powerhouse
Alpine Co.

---

[239] For an explanation of the nickname, see page 171.

Frank Lanterman   Frank D. Lanterman Regional Center
Los Angeles, CA

Lanterman Developmental Center
Pomona, CA

Milton Marks   Senator Milton Marks Branch Library
Milton Marks "Little Hoover" Commission
San Francisco, CA

James R. Mills   James R. Mills Building
Metropolitan Transit Development Board, San Diego

Bob Moretti   Bob Moretti Memorial Scholarship

Bob Moretti Memorial Bench
Capitol Park, Sacramento

Lou Papan   Lou and Irene Papan Lupus Research Program
UC San Francisco

Nicholas Petris   Nicholas C. Petris Lecture
San Francisco State University

Robert Presley   Robert Presley Center for Crime and Justice Studies
UC Riverside

Robert Presley Detention Center
Riverside Co., CA

POST Robert Presley Institute of Criminal Investigation
CSU Sacramento

Richard Polanco   Polanco Fellowship Program
California Latino Caucus Institute

SAFEWAY

LINCOLN SQUARE

SKYLINE TRAVEL
ANTHONY'S SALON
WINES & SPIRITS
BARBER SALON

MAIL CENTER
SKIER'S EDGE
DRY CLEANERS
CVS/Pharmacy

← **ENTER**

CRAFT GALLERY
SALON

Galleria

RED BOY
PIZZA

Since 1969

The Lincoln Square Shopping Center in Oakland (named for Speaker Luther Lincoln).

Jesse Unruh

Jesse M. Unruh Assembly Fellowship Program
Sacramento State University

Rose Ann Vuich

Rose Anne Vuich Ethical Leadership Award
Maddy Institute; CSU Fresno

Massacre Site

Lloyd Magruder Jr.

Magruder Massacre Site[240]
Bitterroot National Forest, Idaho

Duel Site

David Broderick

Broderick Terry Duel Site
California Historical Site No. 19 (Daly City)

Boy Scout Camp

Glenard P. Lipscomb

Camp Lipscomb (Big Bear Lake)

Business

Agoston Haraszthy

Haraszthy Family Cellars
Sonoma, CA

Luther H. Lincoln

Lincoln Square Shopping Center (Oakland)[241]

Edward Tickle

Tickle Pink Inn (Carmel)

---

[240] Magruder and four men who he had hired to help him with a pack-train trip from his home in Lewiston, Idaho to the mines at Adler Ranch, Montana.
[241] The 1957 <u>California Legislature Handbook</u> (California State Printer; 1957) lists Speaker Lincoln's home mailing address as 4000 Redwood Road in Oakland. A neighboring 4100 Redwood Road is now home to the Lincoln Square Shopping Center, including Lincoln Square Liquors.

The Caltrain Engine #923, the "Jackie Speier"
Photo courtesy Caltrain.

Locomotives[242]

Samuel Brannan[243]   California Central/Yuba Railroad #2

John Conness   Central Pacific Railroad #6

Benjamin E. S. Ely   Vaca Valley & Clear Lake Railroad #2

Daniel W. C. Rice   California Pacific Railroad #10

Jackie Speier   Caltrain Engine #925

Train Stations

Alfred Song   Wilshire/Western/Alfred Hoyun Song Station
Los Angeles Metro

Julian C. Dixon   Julian Dixon Metro Rail Station
Los Angeles Metro

Space-related Aircraft

Pete Knight   Scaled Composites White Knight (2002-2014)
Scaled Composites White Knight Two (2008-Present)

---

[242] The author is grateful to Richard Paul for his dedicated efforts as a mentor and countless hours discussing the importance of railroads in California history.
[243] Sources are the Caltrain "Commute Fleets" webpage (caltrain.com/about/statsandreports/commutefleets.html) and the "Table of Names Locomotives of the CP-SP World" by Wendell Huffman (http://cprr.org/Museum/Locomotives/Names_Locomotives.pdf) Accessed December 8, 2016.

Beverages

William T. Boothby[244] Boothby Cocktail

Agoston Haraszthy The Haraszthy Family of Wines
Haraszthy Vineyards (Etyek, Hungary)

The Count (Red Wine)
The Sheriff of Buena Vista (Red Wine)
The Founder (Red Wine)
Buena Vista Winery (Sonoma, CA)

Mariano G. Vallejo M. G. Vallejo Cabernet Sauvignon
M. G. Vallejo Chardonnay
M. G. Vallejo Merlot
M. G. Vallejo Pinot Noir
M. G. Vallejo Zinfandel
M. G. Vallejo Winery (Sonoma, CA)

Abner Weed Abner Weed Pale Ale
Abner Weed Amber Ale
Mount Shasta Brewing Co. (Weed, CA)

Opposite Page: Bottles of The Count and The Sheriff of Buena Vista
Photo courtesy Megan Steffen of Untapped Media Co.

---

[244] William T. Boothby was the author of "Cocktail Boothby's American Bartender: The Only Practical Treatise on the Art of Mixology Published" which was first published in 1891 and reprinted in Anchor Brewing Company in 2007.

Letters from Senator Nelson S. Dilworth to his son Nelson Jr. (1946 to 1960)

Buried History

> "We die not all, for our deeds remain,
> To crown with honor or mar with stain.
> Through endless sequence of years to come,
> Our lives shall speak, though our lips are dumb."
> - *State Senator W. Z. Angney*[245]

Leroy Greene, the ninth longest-serving lawmaker in California, was born in 1918 in Newark, New Jersey. A civil engineer, Greene joined the Army Corps of Engineers during WWII but arrived in Japan after the war had ended. His service in Occupied Japan consisted of evaluating the damage done to infrastructure and the structural stability of damaged buildings.

After the war he moved to California, setting up an office just across an alley from the Governor's Mansion. He was first elected to the State Assembly in 1962 and by the time he retired in 1998, he was the Dean of the State Senate.

When he left office, Greene donated most of his legislative papers to the University Archives at Sacramento State. Many of his personal papers, including a type-written account of his time in Japan and an unpublished autobiography that Greene continued to revise, stayed with him. After he died in 2002, his widow Syma moved many of the old books and filing cabinets out to their garage, where they sat for the next decade.

After Syma died in 2012, the house was cleaned out and prepared for sale. It wasn't until after the property was nearing the end of the escrow that anyone thought to look in the garage. In it were stacks of boxes containing the Senator's personal library and files.

Greene is one of thousands who have served in the California state legislature since 1849, and the story of his papers is similar to many others. One longtime legislator who served from the 1960s to the 1980s

---

[245] History of Santa Clara County by J. P. Munro-Fraser (Alley, Bowen, & Company; 1881), page 592.

stored his writings in a barn just up the rocky hill from his home near Placerville. Another, who served from the 1950s to the 1970s and wrote many of California's landmark mental health laws, entrusted his papers to a former staffer - today these rest in a spare bedroom on the outskirts of Reno.

A third, perhaps suspecting that his work would be of value to future generations, boxed up his papers in an old railcar that had been buried into a hillside on the family ranch. In the case of the papers stored in the railcar, they would remain in the ground for nearly fifty years before the Senator's sons brought them out and moved the collection to their homes for continued storage.

So where should legislative records go after a lawmaker leaves office?

It's an important question and fortunately it has an answer. Since 1850, California has had a State Archives and a State Library to maintain important documents and items related to the history of California.

The California State Archives[246] collects, preserves, and provides access to the historic records of state government including the legislature through its Legislative Archives Program. According to the state's Legislative Open Records Act, they are the official repository for legislative records. In a large and well lit reading room, researchers are able to access the original copies of legislation and notes from the committee staff who analyzed them.

Just one block away is the California State Library, where the state keeps a large share of its publicly-accessible cultural history collection. With more than four million titles including thousands of maps and photographs, the State Library is one of the best places to learn the people and eras that have made the Golden State what it is today. It's a collection that you could easily spend a lifetime exploring.

One particularly interesting items in the library's collection dates back to the first meeting of the legislature in 1850. During the session,

---

[246] The State Archives were created by the very first law ever passed by the legislature (Chapter 1 of 1850).

Assemblyman John S. Bradford asked his fellow lawmakers to take a few moments to write a few short sentences describing their lives: when they had been born, how they had come to California, and where they now lived. Some slipped humor into their entries, like Assemblyman Alexander P. Crittenden, who noted that he was "raised and educated, if at all, in Ohio..."[247]

It's an important history, and should be preserved for future generations. If you have unwanted materials relating to the history of California, please take a moment to contact one of these amazing institutions:

California State Library
900 N Street
Sacramento, CA 95814
(916) 654-0176
cslcal@library.ca.gov

California State Archives
1020 O Street
Sacramento, CA 95814
(916) 653-6814
archivesweb@sos.ca.gov

A legislator license plate used by
Assemblyman Leroy Greene in the 1970s.

---

[247] Crittenden's entry in these papers was also unique in that it held a final note that no other legislator thought to include. His conclusion, "Died _____, 18__", suggested that he knew his words would outlive him.

The State Senate badge for
John Harmer, who died in 2019.

Lawmakers Who Died
Since the Last Edition

"I know some people like to joke when they say things like; "Death is Mother Nature's way of telling you to slow down." Well, that's probably in bad taste, but you can still laugh at it if you like."
- Assemblyman Stan Statham[248]

In the four years since the first edition of this book was published, we've lost a number of former lawmakers. The departed include California's final 1940s legislator, Willard Huyck, who died at nearly 102 years old in 2018. Huyck had not only outlived every other person elected in the 1940s by nearly a decade, but was also the oldest former legislator of all-time.

We also lost our last two 1950s legislators, Bruce Sumner and Jack Holmdahl. Sumner and Holmdahl were both born in 1924 and both had long careers as judges after leaving the legislature. We also lost more recent legislators, including Senator Tom Berryhill and Assemblyman Katcho Achadjian, both of whom died in 2020 just a few years after leaving office.

The departed also included State Senators George C. Deukmejian (who resigned to become Attorney General and later served as Governor) and John Harmer (who resigned to accept an appointment as Ronald Reagan's Lieutenant Governor). On the day the State Senate adjourned in memory of Senator Harmer, I had the opportunity to spend a few minutes speaking with his son Jonny. Speaking of the love that his father had spent decades pouring into his family, I was reminded of something Harmer had written two years after becoming a legislator; "There is no substitute for the investment of time and personal involvement in the lives of children by their parents."[249]

---

[248] "Stan Statham: My take on death" by Stan Statham, Red Bluff Daily News; 12 September 2018.
[249] We Dare Not Fail by John Harmer (Southwest Publishing; 1968)

Richard Hayden, who died in 2017, was one of the first old-time legislators I met when beginning to study the history of the legislature. He served a decade in the State Assembly and left after he accomplished his goal of creating a new community college in his local community. When we spoke in 2004, Hayden told me that when he left office, the board of trustees for the local community college district offered him the position of President of the new campus. He declined the offer, but asked that he be considered for a position teaching an introductory Political Science class. Hayden remained a Political Science instructor at Mission College until his death, teaching about the state he loved.

Stan Statham, a longtime television reporter in Chico, joined the State Assembly in 1976. His years of working as a journalist and appearing on camera had long ago removed any discomfort that he might have felt talking to new people. He was unafraid to try novel ideas, including the idea he is best remembered for; that the best solution for a state that is frequently divided state might be to offer voters a chance at an actual divide.

Lucy Killea was a groundbreaker, serving as a civilian employee of the Army during World War II in a stateside Military Intelligence unit. Later, she served as an analyst for the nascent Central Intelligence Agency. She had a love of California history and served for years on the historic and cultural heritage boards in San Diego. On her final visit to the State Capitol, I asked her if she had any advice to offer a young staffer. I never figured out whether it was her intelligence work or love of history that led to her answer. "Never throw anything away entirely," she told me, "always keep the history files for future use."

Bill Richardson, a Republican legend who founded "Gun Owners of America" while serving in the legislature, died in early 2020. Richardson was a skilled communicator and prolific writer, writing hundreds of articles, speeches, and brochures, as well as a number of books about his experiences in the legislature. As noted earlier in this book, Richardson's What Makes You Think We Read the Bills? (1978) remains one of the most-referred classics for those trying to understand the legislature.

They will be missed.

2017

January 31   **Trice Harvey**
(Assembly 1986-1996)

January 17   **Lucy Killea**
(Assembly 1982-1990, Senate 1990-1996)

March 5   **Anthony C. Beilenson**
(Assembly 1963-1966, Senate 1967-1977)

July 17   **John W. Holmdahl**
(Senate 1959-1966 and 1971-1982)

April 3   **John T. Knox**
(Assembly 1961-1980)

April 10   **Jim Ellis**
(Assembly 1976-1980, Senate 1980-1988)

July 23   **Dave Cogdill**
(Assembly 2000-2006, Senate 2006-2010)

August 4   **Richard D. Hayden**
(Assembly 1971-1980)

August 16   **Ross Johnson**
(Assembly 1978-1995, Senate 1995-2004)

November 21   **March K. Fong Eu**
(Assembly 1967-1974)

2018

March 25	**Bruce Sumner** (Assembly 1957-1962)
May 26	**Paul R. Zeltner** (Assembly 1986-1988)
May 6	**Dr. Sam Aanestad** (Assembly 1998-2002, Senate 2002-2010)
May 8	**George C. Deukmejian** (Assembly 1963-1966, Senate 1967-1979)
July 22	**Paul V. Priolo** (Assembly 1967-1980)
September 5	**Raymond J. Gonzales** (Assembly 1973-1974)
September 23	**W. Craig Biddle** (Assembly 1965-1972, Senate 1972-1974)
September 22	**Robert B. Presley** (State Senate 1974-1994)
October 10	**Thomas M. Hannigan** (Assembly 1978-1996)
October 24	**Don Rogers** (Assembly 1978-1986, Senate 1986-1996)
November 3	**Willard Miller Huyck, Sr.** (Assembly 1947-1950)

2019

January 4   **Gordon Cologne**
(Assembly 1961-1964, Senate 1965-1972)

January 12   **Lawrence Kapiloff**
(Assembly 1973-1982)

March 1   **Paul A. Woodruff**
(Assembly 1988-1994)

April 3   **Winfield Allen Shoemaker**
(Assembly 1965-1968)

July 9   **William E. Dannemeyer**
(Assembly 1963-1978)

August 27   **Wadie P. Deddeh**
(Assembly 1967-1982, Senate 1982-1993)

August 28   **Charles W. Bader**
(Assembly 1982-1990)

September 13   **Paul T. Bannai**
(Assembly 1973-1980)

November 1   **Charles Warren**
(Assembly 1963-1977)

November 28   **Phillip D. Wyman**
(Assembly 1978-1992 and 2001-2002)
(Senate 1993-1994)

December 6   **John L. Harmer**
(Senate 1967-1974)

2020

January 13	**H. L. "Bill" Richardson** (Senate 1967-1988)
February 26	**Peter Clay Frusetta** (Assembly 1994-2000)
March 5	**Katcho Achadjian** (Assembly 2010-2016)
March 27	**Robert J. Campbell** (Assembly 1980-1996)
April 3	**Mike Cullen** (Assembly 1967-1978)
April 15	**John V. Briggs** (Assembly 1967-1977, Senate 1977-1982)
May 15	**Robert C. Cline** (Assembly 1971-1980)
August 1	**Stan Statham** (Assembly 1976-1994)
July 1	**William P. Duplissea** (Assembly 1986-1988)
July 9	**Bruce Nestande** (Assembly 1974-1980)
August 19	**Gwen Moore** (Assembly 1978-1994)
August 29	**Tom Berryhill** (Assembly 2007-2010, Senate 2010-2018)
September 28	**Bruce Bronzan** (Assembly 1982-1992)
October 26	**Jerry Eaves** (Assembly 1984-1992)

Made in the USA
Las Vegas, NV
12 March 2022

45329015R00157